Bulletin 294A—Page 1
Fairmont M19 Car—Series C

Effective December 1, 1935

INSTRUCTIONS
and
SPARE PARTS

Fairmont

INSPECTION CARS

ONE TO FOUR MAN

Class M19 Series C (Battery Ignition)
Class MM19 Series C (Magneto Ignition)

Service Division

FAIRMONT RAILWAY MOTORS, Inc.
FAIRMONT, MINNESOTA, U. S. A.

DISTRICT SALES OFFICES:
Chicago   St. Louis   Washington, D. C.   San Francisco
Fairmont Railway Motors, Ltd., Toronto, Canada

©2010 Periscope Film LLC
All Rights Reserved
www.PeriscopeFilm.com

ISBN # 978-1-935700-23-4

Page 2—Bulletin 294A
Fairmont M19 Car—Series C

TO USERS OF FAIRMONT MOTOR CARS:

FAIRMONT railroad motor cars and engines have an established reputation for dependability, simplicity, and economy. Built to uniform standards, of quality materials, and consistently improved, they are the first choice of those who want maximum performance with minimum upkeep.

The M19 Series C spring mounted steel frame inspection car covered in this book incorporates the results of many years research and field experience. Light and easily handled by one man, it is exceptionally smooth running and amply powered to carry full loads over heavy grades and against head winds.

The general instructions carefully read and followed, will insure excellent service from the M19 Series C car with ordinary care. All important points pertaining to operation and maintenance are fully explained and indexed following for quick reference by operator or repairman.

Upon receipt of this book promptly fill in the car and engine record on page 25, and always mention these factory numbers when writing about the car or ordering parts. Don't give us railroad numbers.

Take good care of this book so it is available for reference when making adjustments and repairs, or ordering spare parts.

TABLE OF CONTENTS

	Page
Air Horn	24
Aluminum Alloy Connecting Rod (instructions)	19
Aluminum Alloy Connecting Rod (spare parts)	28
Aluminum Alloy Piston (instructions)	19, 20
Aluminum Alloy Piston (spare parts)	28
Axles and Axle Bearings (instructions)	11, 12
Axles and Axle Bearings (spare parts)	43, 45
Ball Bearings (instructions)	20, 21
Ball Bearings (spare parts)	31
Battery Ignition (instructions)	16
Battery Ignition (spare parts)	37
Bolts	52
Brake (instructions)	12
Brake (spare parts)	47
Canvas Cover	23
Carbon Deposits	22
Carburetor (instructions)	17, 18
Carburetor (spare parts)	33
Carburetor (control parts)	35
Car Frame and Housing (instructions)	14
Car Identification	25
Cooling System (instructions)	13, 14
Cooling System (spare parts)	29
Crankshaft and Ball Bearings (instructions)	21, 22
Crankshaft and Ball Bearings (spare parts)	31
Cylinder and Crankcase (spare parts)	29
Endless Cord Belt Drive (instructions)	13
Endless Cord Belt Drive (spare parts)	41
Engine Mounting (instructions)	14
Engine Mounting (spare parts)	41
Extension Lift Handles	50
Flywheels (instructions)	20
Flywheels (spare parts)	31
Frame and Deck (spare parts)	49
Fuel System (instructions)	14
Fuel System (spare parts)	32
General Suggestions—Safety First	9
Gongs	24
Headlight (extra equipment)	24, 37
Headlight (spare parts)	37

Bulletin 294A—Page 3
Fairmont M19 Car—Series C

	Page
Housing (spare parts)	51
How the Engine Operates	15
How to Order	25
Insulation (instructions—see wheels)	10
Insulation (spare parts)	43
Loose Wheel (instructions—see wheels)	10
Loose Wheel (spare parts)	43
Lubrication (instructions)	9
Magneto (ball bearing drive parts)	39
Magneto (control parts)	35
Magneto (ignition—extra equipment)	24
Magneto (ignition—see bulletin 202 also)	15
Magneto (installation parts)	38, 39
Magneto (plain bearing drive parts)	39
Mixing Oil and Gasoline	5
Muffler (standard)	29
Muffler (extra equipment)	24
Nuts	52
Oil—Water—Fuel	5
Oil Recommendations	6
Operating the Car	8, 9
Piston and Connecting Rod (instructions)	18, 19
Piston and Connecting Rod (spare parts)	28
Preparing Car for Service	5
Pulleys (instructions)	13
Pulleys (spare parts)	41
Rail Sweeps	24
Reversing Engine (battery ignition)	7
Ringseald Packing (instructions)	22
Ringseald Packing (spare parts)	31, 39
Safety First—General Suggestions	9
Screws	52
Seat Cushion	24
Side Bearing (spare parts)	31
Side Bearing (removal—see crankshaft and ball bearings)	21
Side Seats	23
Sliding Base (instructions)	12, 13
Sliding Base (spare parts)	41
Spark Coil (instructions)	16
Spark Coil (spare parts)	37
Spark Plug (instructions)	17
Spark Plug (see battery ignition equipment)	37
Starting and Stopping Engine (battery ignition)	6, 7
Starting and Stopping Engine (Bosch and Eisemann)	7, 8
Starting and Stopping Engine (Wico equipped)	8
Starting Crank (parts)	31
Step Plates	49
Throttle (instructions)	22
Throttle (control parts)	35
Throttle (spare parts)	29
Thrust Collars (adjustment—see wheel alignment)	11
Thrust Collars (spare parts)	43
Timer (instructions)	17
Timer (spare parts)	35
Tools	37
Washers	52
Water Jacket (spare parts—also see cooling system)	29
Weight and Numerical Part Index	26, 27
Wheels (instructions)	10
Wheels (spare parts)	43
Wheel Alignment	10, 11
Wide Wheel Guards	49
Windshield (extra equipment)	23, 47
Windshield (spare parts)	47

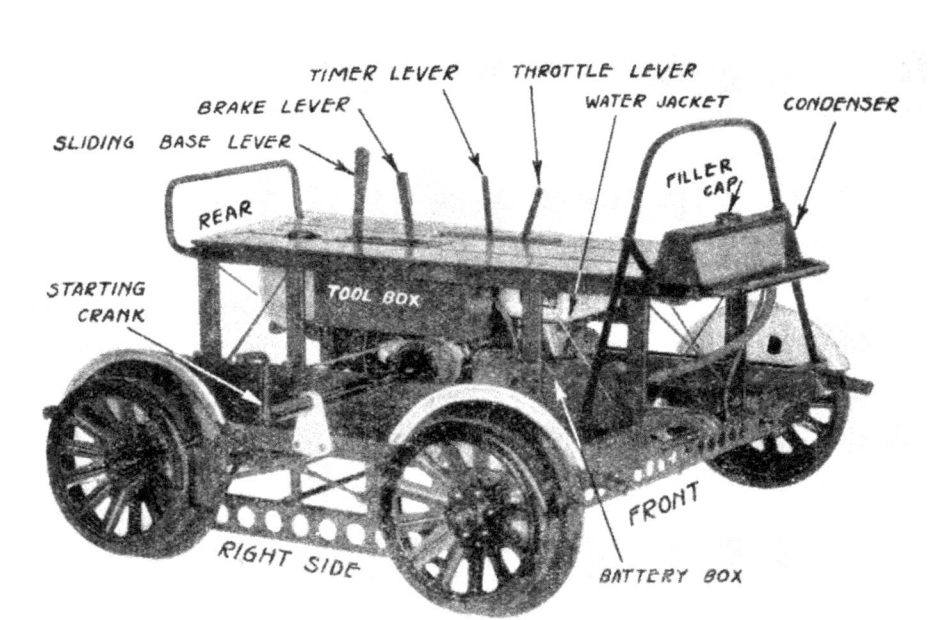

These illustrations show a general view, and the underside of a standard M19 Series C car, with the more important parts pointed out. Reference is frequently made to these parts throughout the bulletin, and the user should thoroughly familiarize himself with them and their functions before placing the car in service or making adjustment and repairs.

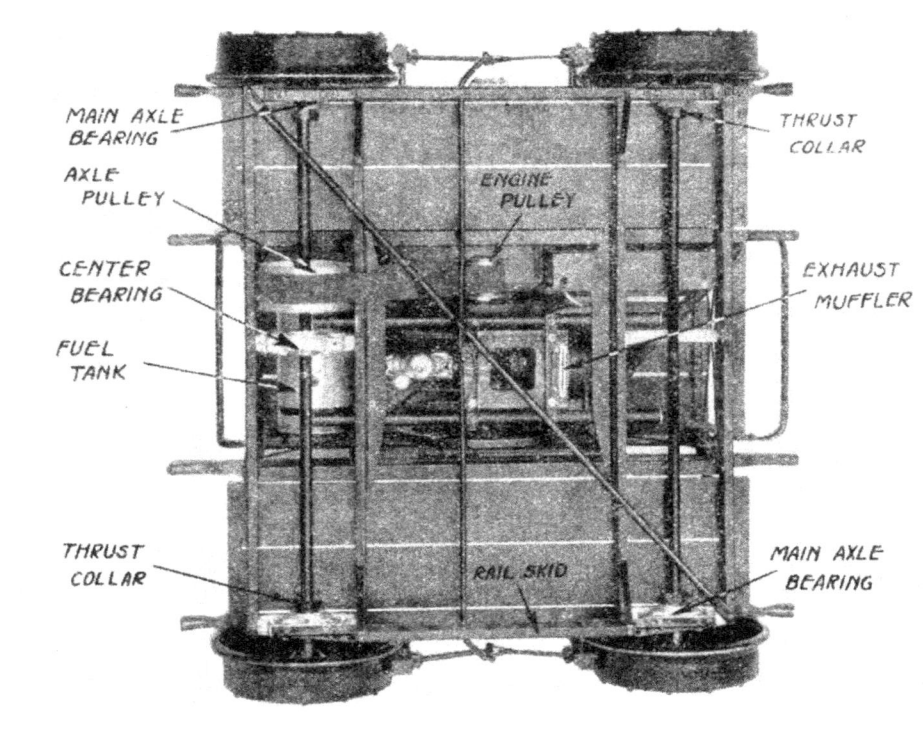

PREPARING CAR FOR SERVICE

Uncrate car, open packing box, and inspect everything for possible damage in transit. If in bad condition make a full report to supervising officials at once.

Open switch on top of car if it has battery ignition, then attach high tension cable to spark plug and connect the loosened wire in battery box. If not sure where to attach this wire see diagram on page 16. On magneto cars it is only necessary to attach high tension cable.

Examine all bolts, nuts and electrical connections for tightness. See that all cotter pins are spread open.

Fill the oil can with the same kind of oil as mixed in the gasoline. Squirt a few drops in each of the five acle bearing oil holes. One is located in the drive axle center bearing. The other four are accessible through openings in outer floor boards. Replace cotters in oil holes to exclude dirt. Oil the loose wheel at the right front of the car.

Oil the two guides in each of the four main axle bearing housings, through holes in aluminum caps bolted to deck side rails. Early cars had short guides stuffed with wicking, and were oiled through small holes in side rails. Also oil drive axle center bearing guides.

Oil the four sliding base bearings and thoroughly work it in by moving the sliding base lever back and forth.

Engine support tubes must slide freely in these bearings. Also oil brake rigging and sliding base lever at working points.

Remove filler cap on top of condenser, open drain cock on left side of water jacket, and pour in clean water up to this level. About six quarts are required. Close cock after water stops running out, and replace filler cap.

Remove the gas tank filler cap through opening in rear of housing and fill tank with oil and gasoline mixed according to instructions on this page, then replace and lock filler cap. Strain this fuel through a fine mesh screen funnel or clean cloth free from lint when filling tank.

Open shutoff valve in fuel line under gas tank. Open drain cock on bottom of carburetor and see that gasoline flows, then close it tight.

The spark and throttle levers stand vertically. The right hand one is the throttle, the left one the timer control.

The carburetor control knob next to brake lever, turns to open or close the needle valve, and pulls up to choke carburetor.

Finally set car on the track and operate the controls to become familiar with them. Release brake, pull sliding base lever back and latch in guide, and see that car rolls freely. Be sure wheels and axles run true, and brake shoes do not drag.

OIL—WATER—FUEL

Satisfactory performance of a motor car depends to a great extent on these three essentials. A FAIRMONT motor car engine of the two-cycle type must not be run without water in the water jacket and lubricating oil thoroughly mixed with the gasoline.

OIL is of vital importance in protecting a motor car and engine against rapid wear. The proper amount and grade of oil must be mixed in the fuel, and bearings and other moving parts must be lubricated regularly.

WATER in the jacket should be kept at the correct level to insure proper engine cooling. When not filled above this level, the jacket will not be damaged by freezing of the water. The simple FAIRMONT cooling system keeps the engine at the most efficient temperature, which insures economical operation.

FUEL can be any standard grade of gasoline. It must be mixed with the correct amount of oil to properly lubricate and operate the FAIRMONT two-cycle engine.

MIXING OIL AND GASOLINE

S. A. E. 30 gas engine or automobile cylinder or will give good results all year 'round. in nearly any climate. We do not recommend the use of an oil heavier than S. A. E. 40. Read "Oil Recommendations" in the next section.

Measure 3/4 pint of oil for each gallon of gasoline (1 part oil and 11 parts gasoline by measue) and stir the mixture thoroughly. Strain through a fine mesh screen funnel or clean cloth free from lint, when filling fuel tank.

Don't use poor oil or reduce the proportions recommended. Never pour oil and gasoline in the tank separately —they will not mix properly. Remember that all internal working parts of the engine are lubricated by the oil mixed in the fuel.

When "breaking in" new engines add 1/4 pint more oil per gallon to the mixture during the first 500 miles of operation, so closely fitted parts wear in smoothly. If gasoline and oil are supplied mixed, add an extra 1/4 pint of oil to each gallon of fuel.

OIL RECOMMENDATIONS

Oils properly refined from either asphalt or paraffine base crudes furnish good lubrication if they do not contain acids, alkalies, and impurities in injurious quantities. In general the lower viscosity oils give cleaner results, and provide a higher factor of safety. Heavy oils have high viscosities and they form excessive carbon and do not flow freely in cold weather.

Engines in which such oils are used quickly carbonize, and hard starting and lack of power result unless carbon deposits are cleaned frequently. Mixing heavy oil in the gasoline in smaller proportions than recommended, reduces the lubricating value of the mixture and lower engine efficiency and higher maintenance costs will result.

FAIRMONT engines are water cooled and the cylinders, pistons, and rings operate at lower temperatures than in air cooled engines. Good lubrication is assured by using oils of suitable viscosity having fairly low pour test. Carbon deposits are also reduced and engines start easier. S. A. E. 30 oils of approximately the following viscosity characteristics are most satisfactory for year 'round use:
At 130° Fahrenheit 185 to 255.
At 210° Fahrenheit 50 to 63.

Oils up to S. A. E. 40 as follows, may be used if S. A. E. 30 is not obtainable.
At 130° Fahrenheit 255 to 450.
At 210° Fahrenheit 62 to 75.

Practically all refiners and oil companies can supply oils conforming to these specifications, and Fairmont Railway Motors, Inc., will gladly render assistance in the selection of lubricants if desired.

STARTING AND STOPPING ENGINE
(Battery Ignition)

The engine will run either forward or backward, but the timer control lever must be set differently for starting and operating in each direction.

STARTING ENGINE FORWARD
(top of flywheels running clockwise or toward water jacket.)

Pull sliding base lever back and latch in guide, and set and lock the brake. Slip starting crank through steady bearing on right side of car, and over the end of crankshaft. Apply a few drops of oil at these places if crank sticks.

TO TEST IGNITION—Retard the spark by moving timer control lever **toward the front** of car as far as it will go. Close switch and slowly crank the engine forward. The coil should buzz only while the timer contact points close. If it buzzes at any other time or does not buzz at all, there may be a short circuit or improperly connected wire, and a check should be made by following instructions on page 16. Finally open switch.

TO PRIME ENGINE—See that shut-off valve at gas tank is open and fuel flows to carburetor. Partly open the throttle by moving lever toward front of car. Open carburetor needle valve 1½ to 2 turns from the closed position by turning control knob to the left.

Be sure ignition switch is open, then spin the engine several times with the crank while pulling up control knob to choke carburetor. This fills the cylinder and crankcase with fresh gas. In cold weather it can also be primed by injecting some of the fuel mixture through the priming cup on throttle valve cover. Choking the carburetor or priming is usually only necessary when starting a new or cold engine.

CRANKING ENGINE—Next release choke control knob, be sure spark is retarded, close switch, and firmly holding the starting crank engaged quickly pull it upward in a clockwise direction. If engine does not start the first time, continue these upward pulls on the crank until it does, priming again if necessary. When the engine starts remove the starting crank. **Never spin the engine with switch on**—injury might result.

IDLING ENGINE—As soon as it starts move the timer control lever toward the rear of the car to advance the spark, and slightly close throttle so engine runs slowly until it warms up, then set carburetor needle valve to the best running position, about 3/4 to 1 turn open.

Never "race" a cold engine to warm it up, nor run it at high speed when the car is standing. The aluminum piston will expand faster than the cylinder and these parts are liable to seize and score.

TO STOP ENGINE open the switch. Just before it stops turning open the throttle to fill the engine with fresh gas and make starting easier next time.

(Continued on following page.)

(Continued from preceding page.)

STARTING ENGINE BACKWARD
(top of flywheels running anticlockwise or away from water jacket.)

Retard the spark by moving timer lever **toward the rear** of car as far as it will go.

Follow the preceding instructions for testing ignition, setting throttle, priming, and starting, but crank the engine anticlockwise or backward.

As soon as it starts, move the timer lever toward the front of the car to advance the spark, and after warming up set needle valve to proper running position.

TO STOP ENGINE open switch and then the throttle, to fill the engine with fresh gas.

REVERSING ENGINE
(Battery Ignition)

To reverse a battery engine when running, without using starting crank, the belt must be free.

Open ignition switch and leave timer set in advance position. Open throttle as engine slows down. Just before flywheels stop turning, close switch and engine will kick back and run in the opposite direction.

Then advance the spark for this reverse direction by properly setting timer lever, and close throttle so engine idles.

Magneto ignition engines cannot be reversed in this way.

STARTING AND STOPPING ENGINE
(Bosch or Eisemann Magneto Equipped)

Cars and engines equipped with these magnetos have the same throttle control as battery types, but no timer lever or switch. The magneto is timed so an engine can be run in either direction. The spark is "fixed" or permanently set, there being no "advance" or "retard."

The magneto is controlled by a rod attached to the magneto interrupter arm, and extending from the lower middle of the housing on the left side of the car. The interrupter can be moved to its two extreme positions, by pushing or pulling this rod.

Thoroughly study magneto bulletin 202 attached, in addition to the following.

STARTING ENGINE FORWARD
(top of flywheels running clockwise or toward water jacket.)

FOR STARTING ENGINE FORWARD the control rod must be pushed in as far as it will go. This turns on the ignition.

TO STOP ENGINE RUNNING FORWARD the control rod is pulled out until the magneto interrupter arm stands vertically. This cuts off the ignition.

Pull sliding base lever back and latch in guide, and set and lock the brake. Slip starting crank through steady bearing on right side of car, and over the end of crankshaft. Apply a few drops of oil at these places if crank sticks.

TO PRIME ENGINE—See that shut-off valve at gas tank is open and fuel flows to carburetor. Partly open the throttle by moving lever toward front of car. Open carburetor needle valve 1½ to 2 turns from the closed position by turning control knob to the left.

Set magneto control rod to **cut off ignition** as already instructed, before cranking forward. Then spin the engine **forward** or clockwise several times with the crank while pulling up control knob to choke carburetor. This fills the cylinder with fresh gas. In cold weather it can also be primed by injecting some of the fuel mixture through the priming cup on throttle valve cover.

TO START ENGINE FORWARD after priming, release the choke and **push** control rod in as far as it will go to turn on ignition.

Firmly holding the crank in place give a quick upward pull in a forward or clockwise direction. If the engine does not fire the first time continue these upward pulls on the crank until it does. **Never spin the engine with the magneto set for starting**—injury might result.

IDLING ENGINE—As soon as it starts remove the starting crank and slightly close the throttle so engine runs slowly until it warms up, then set carburetor needle valve to the best running position, about ¾ to 1 turn open.

Never "race" a cold engine to warm it up, nor run it at high speed when the car is standing. The aluminum piston will expand faster than the cylinder and these parts are liable to seize and score.

(Continued on page 8.)

(Continued from page 7.)

TO STOP ENGINE WHEN RUNNING FORWARD—Pull the magneto control rod out until the magneto interrupter arm stands vertically. Just before engine stops open the throttle to fill the engine with fresh gas and make starting easier next time.

STARTING ENGINE BACKWARD

(top of flywheels running anti-clockwise or away from water jacket.)

FOR STARTING ENGINE BACKWARD the control rod must be pulled out as far as it will come. This turns on the ignition.

TO STOP ENGINE RUNNING BACKWARD the control rod is pushed in until the magneto interrupter arm stands vertically. This cuts off the ignition.

TO PRIME ENGINE—Prepare the car as explained previously, but set magneto control rod to **cut off ignition** as already instructed before cranking backward. Then spin the engine **backward** or anti-clockwise several times with the crank while choking carburetor, to fill the cylinder with fresh gas.

TO START ENGINE BACKWARD after priming, release choke and **pull** control rod out as far as it will come to turn on ignition. Crank the engine backwards or anti-clockwise by quick upward pulls. **Never spin it with the magneto set for starting**—injury might result.

Follow previous instructions for idling and warning up the engine.

TO STOP ENGINE WHEN RUNNING BACKWARD—Push the magneto control rod in until the magneto interrupter arm stands vertically, and open the throttle to fill engine with fresh gas and make starting easier next time.

STARTING AND STOPPING ENGINE
(Wico Magneto Equipped)

Cars and engines equipped with Wico LD1 magnetos have the same throttle control as battery types, and either a switch or push button in the ignition circuit. The switch must be closed, or the push button held down, to cut off the ignition.

These magnetos are timed so an engine can be run in either direction. There is no magneto control as the reversible impulse coupling automatically retards the spark while starting, and advances it when the engine is running.

Partly open throttle and make the same preparations for starting as with other engines, then **close** the switch or **hold down** the push button to **cut off** the ignition. Spin the engine several times with the crank in either direction while choking carburetor, to fill the cylinder with fresh gas.

Then release choke, turn on ignition by opening switch or releasing push button, and crank the engine in the desired direction by pulling upward on the starting crank.

After the engine starts close the throttle so it runs slowly until warmed up, then set carburetor needle valve to best running position, about ¾ to 1 turn open.

OPERATING THE CAR

HANDLING CAR

Pull out extension lift handles when setting car on and off the track. The rail skids assist in handling over high rails. Be careful not to strike axle pulley on rails. Avoid dropping car on rail skids, or off rails when removing from track. Use care in setting off at crossings, switches and frogs so axles are not sprung by pinching wheels in flangeways.

STARTING THE CAR

Always drive with the engine ahead in normal service and on long trips. After starting and warming up the engine seat passengers on the car, operator facing ahead, and release brake.

Then gradually open the throttle to increase power, and at the same time tighten the belt by slowly releasing the sliding base lever. This allows the belt to slip and act as a clutch while the engine picks up the load.

After the car gets under way, fully release the sliding base lever. Then regulate car speed by opening and closing the throttle.

DRIVING THE CAR

Always drive a new car slowly and carefully until thoroughly familiar with the controls. A speed of 15 to 20 miles per hour for the first 500 miles is recommended.

Keep the sliding base tension springs adjusted just tight enough to prevent belt slippage when driving. The adjusting wing nuts at the front end of sliding base tubes should be secured with lock wires after proper belt tension adjustment is made. For average conditions the spark should be well advanced, and the throttle set to maintain proper traveling speed. This insures full power from the engine and economical operation.

If the car loses speed or the engine knocks on hard pulls with open throttle, give the spark more retard, and slip the belt a little if necessary. When coasting down light grades the belt can be released and throttle closed, thereby saving fuel and cooling the engine. In descending heavy grades the engine can be used as a brake by leaving belt tight, closing throttle, and cutting off ignition, also using car brake if needed.

When making a brief stop leave the engine running, so the car can be started again without cranking the engine.

STOPPING THE CAR

First close the throttle, then retard the spark part way.

Next pull sliding base lever back and latch in guide plate to release belt, and apply the brake.

Shut off ignition to stop the engine if car is to be removed from the track.

REVERSING THE CAR

To reverse a battery ignition car without cranking, release belt and bring car to a full stop, allowing the engine to run slowly. Then reverse the engine as explained on page 7, after which the car can be driven in the other direction.

The reversing feature permits running back to setoffs, making inspections, etc., but the car should not be driven backward for long distances. Always operate the engine and condenser ahead on long trips.

A magneto equipped car cannot be reversed in this way. The engine must be stopped and cranked in the opposite direction.

LUBRICATION

The same grade of oil that is mixed in the gasoline is satisfactory for general lubication of the car.

Always mix ¾ pint of oil with each gallon of gasoline. This mixture lubricates all internal moving parts of the engine.

Once a month unscrew the plug in the belt side bearing on the engine and oil the outboard ball bearing well. Be sure no grit or foreign matter enters. Screw plug back tight.

Once a week apply a few drops of oil through the oil holes in the four main axle bearings and in the drive axle center bearing.

Oil the axle bearing guides daily.

Once a week apply a few drops of oil to the four sliding base bearings.

Oil the loose wheel frequently to prevent its sticking.

Occasionally oil working points of sliding base lever and brake rigging.

GENERAL SUGGESTIONS—SAFETY FIRST

Careful observance of the following and study of this instruction book will insure a long lived dependable motor car and a clean safety record.

Inspect the car before starting out each day, and make sure it is in good operating condition.

Once a week clean the entire car thoroughly, examining gasoline joints, electrical connections, bolts, screws, etc., and tighten all loose parts.

When making inspection see that:
(1) Wheel tire bolts are tight.
(2) Wheel tires are not worn dangerously thin at flange or on tread.
(3) Wheels and axles run true.
(4) Axle end nuts are secured by cotters.
(5) All wheels except loose one are tight on axles.
(6) Loose wheel is not worn too loose on bushing.

Keep engine and axle pulleys aligned so the belt runs true, and does not rub pulley flanges or flywheel.

Keep the brake adjusted and in first class working condition.

Lubricate all moving parts regularly.

Don't "race" the engine at high speed when car is standing.

Handle car on and off the rails carefully to avoid damage.

If car must stand outside in bad weather protect it with a fireproof canvas cover.

Don't overload the car—maximum capacity is 750 lbs. at ordinary speeds.

Load baggage and tools carefully to prevent their working into moving parts or falling under the car and causing an accident.

Drive slowly with car under full control where there is not a clear view ahead, over road crossings, through gangs of workmen, through railroad yards, and over frogs and switches.

Don't drive during rain or snow storms or foggy weather unless necessary, and then only with a lineup and extra precaution.

When following other motor cars or trains remain 500 feet or more behind.

If car is run at night protect it with proper signal lights at front and rear.

Keep fire and lights away from gasoline tank and carburetor.

Above all, adhere strictly to local railroad motor car rules.

WHEELS

Standard M19 series C cars use 17"x¼" two-piece pressed steel wheels, with malleable hubs riveted in place. Three wheels are mounted on the tapered axle ends with fiber bushings in the hubs and fiber washers next to the outer hub faces to provide electrical insulation. The group is drawn tight by the axle end nut and a steel washer.

The loose wheel at front on right side, is straight bored and mounted on a bronze bushing. A few drops of oil daily insures proper operation. Keep this bushing just tight enough on the axle to prevent its turning. Never operate car when loose wheel is a sloppy fit on bushing.

Each wheel tire is tightly held on the hub and disc assembly by twelve heat-treated stretch proof bolts. Removing these bolts and swinging the brake shoe clear, permits of quickly exchanging a tire without taking the complete wheel off the axle. Common bolts must not be substituted for the heat treated ones, as they will stretch and tires will loosen.

To remove an insulated wheel or hub and disc assembly, take off axle end nut and screw an M8705 shock wheel puller on the axle until it seats tight. Strike the end of the puller several sharp blows with a heavy hammer, at the same time prying between the car frame and wheel hub.

The loose wheel can be slipped off after end nut and steel washer have been removed. Jar bronze bushing off with shock puller while prying between frame and bushing shoulder.

Before applying a wheel or a hub and disc assembly be sure the axle runs true. Before applying insulation smooth all burrs in the wheel hub and wipe the bore clean. Then carefully drive insulating bushing in until flush with the outer face; and tighten wheel on the axle with end nut and steel washer, being sure the fiber washer is next to outer hub face. If wheels come too close together (under gauge) tough paper can be wrapped around the bushing. If too far apart (over gauge) slightly ream the bushing with M7666 taper reamer. Be sure insulated wheels are tight on the taper and all wheels run true.

Drive wheel's must be approximately the same size. They can be measured with a steel tape around the tread, being careful to keep it equidistant from the flanges at all points. Sometimes small differences in their circumferences cause a car to run to one side when perfectly aligned.

WHEEL ALIGNMENT

NOTE—Sometimes a small difference in drive wheel circumferences causes a car to run to one side even though perfectly aligned. Again, another car will operate satisfactorily with drive wheels showing more variation. Track conditions, direction of wind, car loading, and windshield have more or less effect on a car, and it may tend to run to one side even when in alignment.

Careful observance of these instructions insures a safe running car. This diagram represents the running gear of any motor car, but the instructions apply only to the M19 series C cars with 17" pressed steel wheels.

(1) Replace bent or sprung frame members if any, and check frame for squareness. Measurements "G" across corners should be the same if frame is square. Finally tighten all frame bolts and nuts.

(2) Carefully block up under the car frame so all wheels turn freely and frame is level.

(3) Examine wheels and replace tires or wheels with badly worn flanges.

(4) Drive wheel tires must be approximately the same size. Measure them with a steel tape around the tread, being careful to keep it equidistant from the flanges at all points.

(5) (a) Rotate wheel and axle assembly, and hold a piece of chalk steady so it just touches outer face of each wheel. If wheel and axle run true chalk will mark evenly around wheel—if wheel is sprung or axle is bent chalk will mark the high spot on wheel. Wheels or axles badly out of true usually must be replaced, though axles can sometimes be straightened. A maximum tolerance of $\frac{1}{32}$" out of true is recommended on wheel tread, and up to $\frac{1}{16}$" out of true on wheel face or flange.

(b) Another method of check is with a straight edge or two-foot carpenter's square across outer wheel faces (see diagram). Mark each tire face in quarters and measure from the square to the side rail at each quarter. The measurements should be the same for each wheel, if the wheel and axle run true.

(6) Axle center distance "A" should be the same on both sides of car. Axle bearing support bolts can be loosened to permit shifting the wheel and axle

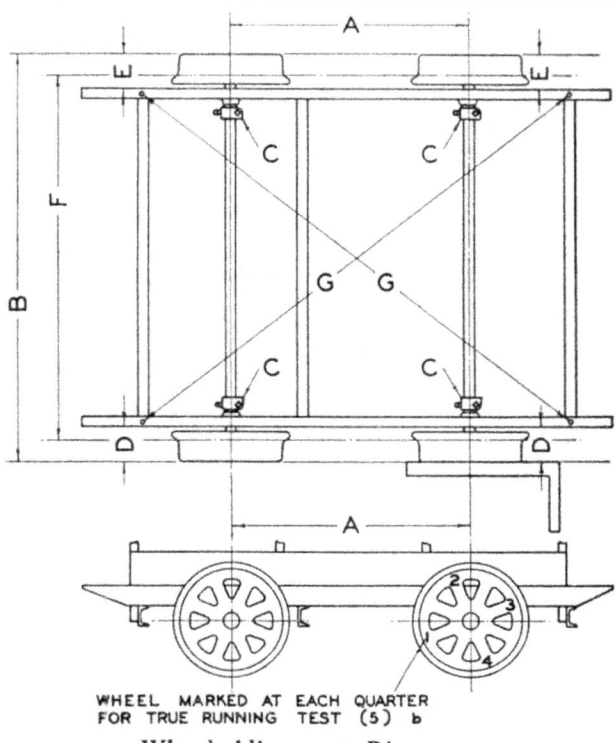

WHEEL MARKED AT EACH QUARTER FOR TRUE RUNNING TEST (5) b

Wheel Alignment Diagram.

assemblies a trifle. If necessary replace worn parts, such as bearing supports and casings.

(7) A tolerance of $\frac{1}{16}$" over or $\frac{1}{8}$" under gauge "F" is recommended. The measurement over the outside faces of wheels at "B" is $62\frac{13}{16}$" when M19 series C 17" wheels are exactly to $56\frac{1}{2}$".

gauge. Both axle assemblies must measure the same to properly align wheels.

(8) New insulating bushings are sometimes necessary to bring wheels to gauge. These must be carefully fitted so wheels run true. If loose wheel and loose wheel bushing are badly worn, both may have to be replaced.

(9) With frame approximately centered between the four wheels, the outside faces of left wheels should be in line and parallel with left side rail. Check with a straight edge, tight cord, or carpenter's square, being sure distances "E" are both the same. If necessary loosen and shift thrust collars "C" to align these wheels.

(10) Next check right side of car where distances "D" should also be equal and approximately the same as "E".

(11) Carefully set all thrust collars "C" against axle bearings, being sure lugs engage in slots. First tighten clamp bolts, then set screws and lock nuts.

(12) After thrust collars are set, make another check of wheels to be sure alignment has not been disturbed.

AXLES AND BEARINGS

The alloy steel axles run on Bower bearings at each end, and a Hyatt steady bearing supports the drive axle next to the pulley.

The axle bearings are enclosed in oil tight and dust proof casings. A few drops of oil in each casing through the oil hole once a week provides sufficient lubrication. Use the same kind of oil that is mixed in the gasoline. Also oil the Hyatt steady bearing at the same time.

When general overhauling or extensive repairs require the removal of axles and bearing assemblies, disconnect brake rigging and take off wheels, then the side rails. Unbolt rail skids, and bearing supports from cross channels, permitting the removal of main axle bearings. The drive axle with pulley and center bearing may be slipped out toward the rear after removing rear cross channel, and bolts securing the center bearing.

For lighter repairs such as replacing bent axles, proceed as above but remove side rail, rail skid, and bearing assemblies from right side only. Then pull axle out of bearing on opposite side. When removing drive axle in this manner, loosen bolts in axle pulley and wedge the hub open enough to permit pulling the axle through.

The bearings can be jarred out of casings after removing the riveted covers. Wash all parts clean and inspect them whenever removed from the axle. When reassembling rollers and races, oil them well and be sure to have beveled edge of outer race against beveled flanges of the rollers. These surfaces carry the side thrust of car and must run together.

The Hyatt center bearing should also be cleaned and oiled whenever the drive axle is removed.

Two thrust collars on each axle take up end play. To adjust a thrust

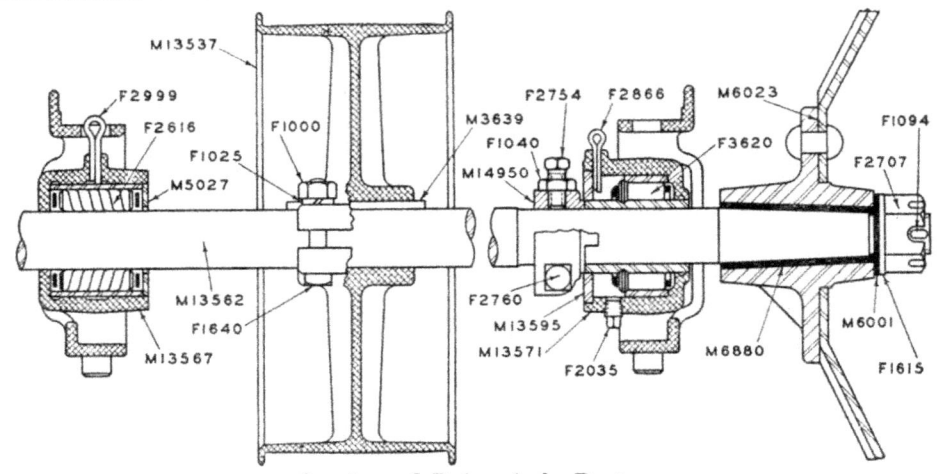

Section of Drive Axle Parts.

collar loosen set screw and clamp bolt, then tap collar snugly against axle bearing. Driving lugs on collar must be in the slots in bearing race. When correctly set, tighten clamp bolt first, then set screw, and finally lock nut. Be sure wheels are in alignment when thrust collars are finally set.

A slightly sprung axle can usually be straightened cold, but one badly bent should be replaced at once. Never heat alloy steel axles when straightening, as the steel will be weakened.

BRAKE

To bring the car to a quick stop apply the brake with firm steady pressure, yet allowing the wheels to revolve. If applied suddenly, or too hard, the wheels may lock and slide on the rails.

Go over the brake when weekly car inspection is made, and tighten bolts and adjust shoes if necessary. Be sure cotter pins are spread. Remember a car is no safer than the brake.

To adjust brake, disconnect adjustable toggles (one on each side of car). Unscrew the yoke on each toggle 3 or 4 turns, then reconnect parts. Try the brake and if necessary make further adjustment until all four shoes take hold on the wheels at the same time. Also be sure the lever can be latched in the first notch in the guide plate.

Suspension of the brake shoes on hanger links insures maximum brake efficiency, as the full face of each liner bears on the wheel when the brake is applied. Replacement liners should be installed when the steel faces of the old ones wear through. Be sure liners and bolts securing them do not touch other brake parts, as electric signals might be operated.

Each brake shoe on late cars is firmly held between the hanger links by a friction spring and long hanger pin. These parts are applicable to early cars which used short hanger pins without friction springs.

SLIDING BASE

The engine supports are mounted on tubes that slide in bearings bolted to car frame. Inside each tube is a heavy coiled spring, anchored at rear end and carrying a stud and wing nut on front end. These sliding tubes telescope inside the front end tension tubes. Tightening the wing nuts draws support tubes forward and holds engine into belt.

To release belt, pull sliding base lever back and latch it in notch in guide plate. When lever is unlatched for driving car, it must not bear against front end of slot or belt will slip. Check this by lightly pulling back on lever when car is being driven. It should clear slot end by at least an inch.

The lever is adjusted by turning the pull rod adjuster wing nut. With engine shut off, adjust so that lever pulls back about four inches from front end of slot before moving engine. When lever is latched in notch the belt should not drag on pulleys.

The endless cord belt has very little stretch, and after the first few adjustments it settles to its permanent length. Then pull rod adjuster and belt require little attention.

Bulletin 294A—Page 13
Fairmont M19 Car—Series C

If belt slips when lever is properly adjusted, tighten wing nuts just enough to prevent slipping. Too much tension shortens belt life. If necessary to remove sliding base tubes or bearings, loosen the wing nuts.

ENDLESS CORD BELT DRIVE

Always leave the belt slack when car is not in use. The endless cord belt is "endless" and it must not be cut or laced. Properly cared for it will give many thousands of miles service. Never use belt dressing on the belt.

If the belt glazes over and slippage cannot be overcome by increasing spring tension, scrub the inner belt face with a rag saturated in gasoline from the fuel tank. Also clean pulley faces, then dust a little tire talc or powdered soapstone on belt and pulleys before operating car.

To change belts: Release sliding base lever and turn adjuster wing nut tight so as to obtain maximum belt release when lever is again latched, then run belt off engine pulley. Raise the rear of car about a foot and securely block up under No. 3 cross channel.

Remove the right rear tool tray block and four bolts which secure floor boards to No. 3 and No. 4 cross channels on the right side of car. Take out remaining bolts that hold right side rail, remove one brake toggle link pin, and swing rear end of rail (with wheel guards and brake parts attached) upward in the clear.

Remove rear center bearing bolt, two bolts holding sway brace and rail skid brace to No. 3 cross channel, two housing bolts through No. 3 and No. 4 cross channels on right side, and bolts holding rail skid and rear cross channel to right rear bearing support.

Pull back the right end of No. 4 channel. Slip belt off axle pulley and through this opening between channel and bearing, also along top of No. 3 channel and between rail skid and bearing support and finally around wheel. Apply new one and reassemble in reverse order.

Measure axle center distance on both sides, being sure it is equal. See paragraph 6 on page 10. Adjust sliding base lever as instructed on page 12.

PULLEYS

The engine pulley is held on the flywheel by three cap screws which must be kept tight. If these screws are removed, or replaced with others, be sure lock washers are used under the heads and that screws are flush with the pulley lugs, or the belt will be damaged by projecting ends.

The axle pulley is clamped in place and driven by a key. Keep the clamp bolts in the hub tight so the pulley does not shift out of alignment. In handling the car on and off the rails be careful not to damage the axle pulley.

Keep the pulleys in line at all times so the belt runs true and does not rub the flanges or climb over them.

COOLING SYSTEM

Use clean soft water in the water jacket if it is available. Check the water regularly and keep it up to the water level cock. Capacity of the system is six quarts.

Unlike an automobile radiator, the condenser is not filled with water. Instead, steam from boiling water in the jacket passes through upper hose into the condenser where it is condensed to water which drains back through lower hose into the jacket. This maintains a supply of water in the engine, and insures uniform temperature and economy of operation.

If there are no leaks in the cooling system and the car is driven with condenser ahead, the water supply will provide ample cooling for average conditions. When the car is driven hard in unusually hot weather, or backward for long distances, some water will have to be added. After long service, lime and scale deposits from the water may cause overheating. These can be scraped off the cylinder walls after removing the jacket and head.

A motor car operated in severe cold weather may cool too much, or the condenser may fill with frost causing water to be forced out thru the overflow. To insure normal operation, partially or entirely cover the front of the condenser with cardboard or canvas. This protection should be varied according to temperature conditions, and entirely removed on warm days.

Cars can stand in freezing weather without harm to the jacket, providing water is not carried above the proper level. If filled too full, the jacket may be damaged by freezing. Before operating a car with frozen water in the jacket, run the engine slowly for a few minutes to thaw ice around the cylinder and in drain hose. Do not move engine back and forth with ice in drain hose.

For easiest starting in cold weather, drain water at night and refill with hot water the next morning.

Many operators use anti-freeze mixtures during the winter months. While these have little or no effect on the starting of a cold engine, they do have an advantage in that they do not freeze like water.

Automobile anti-freeze mixtures which contain mineral salts must not be used, as they corrode the aluminum jackets and soldered joints.

Mixtures of alcohol and water give fair satisfaction in severe weather, providing the condenser is not covered. Under these conditions the alcohol which boils at a lower temperature than water, is condensed and drained back to the jacket without loss and there is little danger of frost forming in the condenser. There will however be more or less loss of alcohol from the mixture at temperatures near freezing and above, or if the condenser is covered.

Equal parts of water, and radiator glycerine or Prestone make a satisfactory anti-freeze, providing the condenser is protected to prevent frost forming inside. They may freeze slushy in severe weather, but quickly thaw when the engine is started. Glycerine or Prestone must not be used without water as their high boiling points will result in damage to the engine. Always use water to replenish any loss by evaporation.

FUEL SYSTEM

Inspect the fuel system regularly and see that the tank is securely held by the tank straps. At least once a year, oftener if necessary, remove the tank from the car and thoroughly flush it out to remove sediment, water, and lint.

Leaks at fuel pipe couplings can usually be stopped by tightening the brass nuts snugly. If this does not overcome leakage cut off the ends of fuel pipe just back of the old sleeves, and apply new F3030 compression sleeves with the pipe extending about ⅛" through them. Then tighten coupling nuts firmly to seat all parts together.

The F3613 gas tank cap has an air vent to allow free flow of fuel to the carburetor. Never use an F5115 condenser cap on the gas tank as it has no vent and will cause fuel trouble.

Loops and bends in the fuel pipe sometimes cause "air locks" which prevent the flow of gasoline. Blowing in the tank will start the flow if fuel pipe is not clogged.

The carburetor strainer bowl should be taken off and cleaned at least once a month, oftener in winter to prevent freezing of accumulated water. Be sure gaskets are in good condition when replacing bowl.

Don't use heavy wrenches on fuel pipe couplings or carburetor bowl.

CAR FRAME AND HOUSING

The car frame is assembled from steel channels and angles, and oak floor boards securely bolted together. This construction, with the long diagonal sway brace provides maximum strength and rigidity and maintains alignment. Keep all frame bolts tight. In case members become damaged straighten them, or if badly out of shape replace.

To remove the complete housing from car, close gasoline shutoff valve and disconnect fuel line and choke wire at carburetor. Drain water jacket and disconnect both hoses from engine. On battery cars disconnect the two wires from timer and one each from battery and coil. On magneto cars disconnect magneto control rod.

Pull sliding base lever back, block between engine and No. 2 cross channel, then release sliding base and brake levers. Remove cotters and slotted nuts from the 8 housing chassis bolts, also two machine bolts holding front safety rail to floor end blocks, and lift housing off.

ENGINE MOUNTING

Engines used on M19 series C cars are designated as O and OM. They are secured to the engine supports by four bolts with lock washers and hex nuts.

With the complete housing lifted from car, the engine is accessible for any repairs. If it is to be removed from the frame, loosen sliding base tension wing nuts, then unbolt and lift it out. Always use lock washers when reassembling.

HOW THE ENGINE OPERATES

The top view below shows the piston passing over the exhaust and intake ports, as it moves toward the cylinder head and compresses fresh gases in the cylinder. At the same time it creates a vacuum in the crankcase, opening the carburetor check valve and air valve, through which fresh gases are drawn into the crankcase.

rush through them into the cylinder. The deflector on the piston sweeps these fresh gases toward the cylinder head and spark plug, forcing the remaining burnt gases out through the exhaust ports.

As the flywheels and crankshaft turn, the piston starts back toward the cylinder head on another "compression

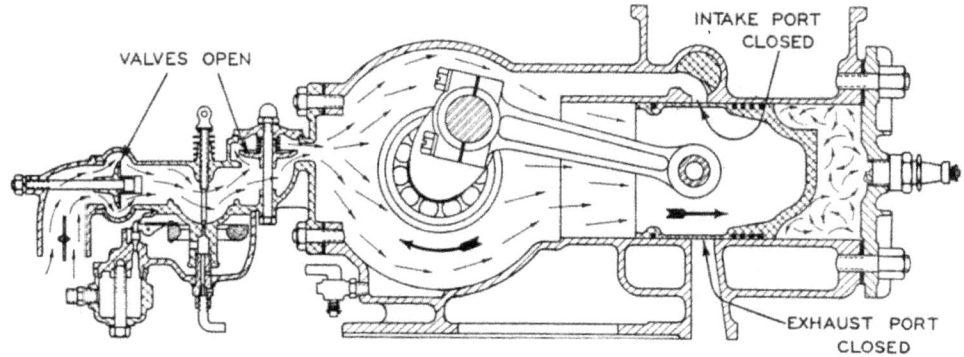

Compression Stroke

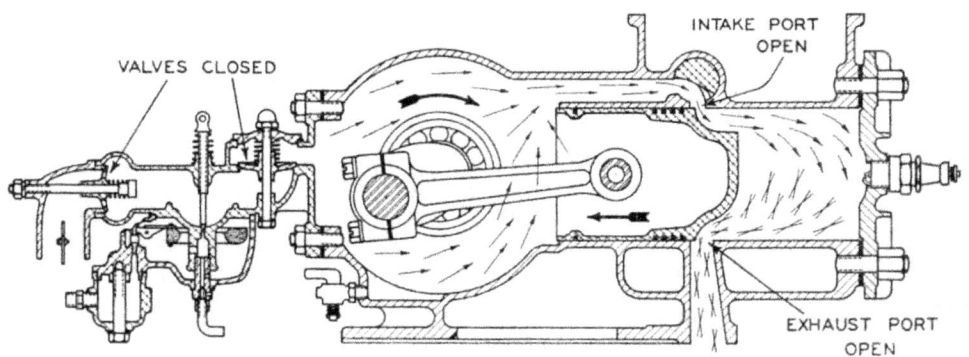

Power Stroke

When the piston reaches the end of this "compression stroke" the spark at the spark plug ignites the compressed gases, and expansion of the burning mixture drives the piston away from the cylinder head. As the piston moves away the carburetor valves close, and gases in the crankcase are compressed.

The lower view shows the piston nearing the end of this "power stroke" where it first uncovers the exhaust ports, and burnt gases start to escape. Immediately afterward the piston also uncovers the intake ports, and fresh compressed gases from the crankcase

stroke" and again covers the ports. The fresh gases are again compressed, ignited, expanded, and exhausted. This same cycle of events is repeated over and over rapidly when the engine runs.

The FAIRMONT engine runs equally well in either direction, has no valves in the combustion chamber, and delivers a power impulse at every revolution. It is far more powerful for its size and weight than the four cycle type, and having comparatively few moving parts it can be maintained more economically.

MAGNETO IGNITION

The magneto which furnishes ignition on magneto engines is a self-contained unit connected to the spark plug by one wire. See bulletin 202 for instructions on magneto maintenance and magneto spare parts.

BATTERY IGNITION

A battery ignition system includes four dry cells to supply current, and a coil which transforms this current to a jump spark, both carried in the battery box, and wired to the timer on the engine which closes and opens the electrical circuit at the proper time. A switch on top of the car cuts off or turns on the ignition. This switch must always be open when working on the engine or not using the car.

An engine which misses when cold and first started, will usually fire regularly after being warmed up. Therefore before changing ignition system adjustments to overcome such missing, always drive the car until warmed up and try different carburetor adjustments.

Then if ignition is suspected of causing the trouble check all wiring, switch and connections to be sure there are no loose connections, or broken or bare wires. Sometimes wires which appear to be good are broken inside the insulation. A wire suspected of being broken should be replaced with a new piece. Scrape all wires and connections clean and tighten with pliers. Coil connections should be lightly tightened to prevent twisting wires loose inside the coil.

The wiring of the M19 Series C is shown in the diagram above. The "ground" wire from the lower terminal of the timer connects to the switch blade. Wiring should be kept free from oil, gasoline, and water, as they rot the insulation and weaken the ignition.

New dry cells test 30 to 35 amperes each and a set is good for several

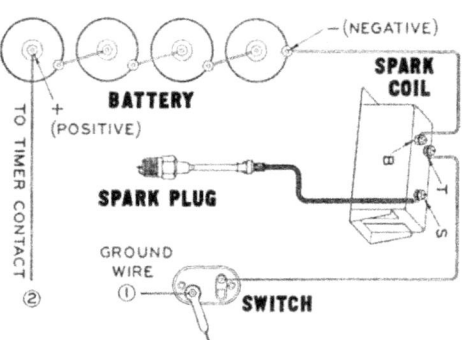

Battery Ignition Wiring

months' service. Usually they furnish good ignition until exhausted to 8 or 10 amperes each, when the entire set should be replaced and connected according to the diagram. Never use cells which test less than 6 to 8 amperes after standing unused for several hours.

Freezing reduces the efficiency of dry cells and they require replacement more often in cold weather than in summer. In severely cold weather they can be taken inside over night to prevent freezing, and they will then deliver full current for starting next morning.

The inside of the battery box must be kept dry, and dry cells must be firmly clamped or wedged in place so they do not shift and permit connections to touch each other. Never remove cardboard cases from dry cells, or lay tools on them in the battery box.

SPARK COIL

Keep the spark coil dry at all times and never connect more than four dry cells to it. When the ignition system is in good working condition a ¼" to 5/16" spark should jump from the end of the high tension cable to the engine. If the coil will not deliver this spark the vibrator points may require attention, or a new coil may be necessary.

Turning the coil adjusting nuts to the right tightens the vibrator and produces a hotter spark, but also increases current consumption. Turning them to the left loosens the vibrator and reduces the spark. Keep the vibrator adjusted as loosely as possible without causing the engine to miss—this lengthens battery life and prevents burning the points.

The platinum alloy vibrator points should be dressed clean and smooth with a fine file, pocket stone, or emery cloth, when they become rough or pitted. After these points wear thin a complete new vibrator F4166 should be fitted on the coil. Always see that points match and seat together evenly after dressing them, or when fitting a new vibrator.

Inferior tungsten point vibrators reduce the efficiency of the ignition system, and they should not be used.

Bulletin 294A—Page 17
Fairmont M19 Car—Series C

SPARK PLUG

To test the spark plug, remove it from the engine and lay on some metallic part of the car frame or engine, with high tension cable attached. Close switch and slowly turn engine until timer contacts close and the coil buzzes. If the spark at the plug gap is not steady while the coil buzzes, check the high tension cable for defects and clean the plug, then test again. If the spark plug porcelain is cracked or suspected of being defective, replace the plug with one known to be in good condition.

Set plug points at $\frac{1}{32}$" gap for battery ignition and $\frac{1}{64}$" for magneto ignition. They should be checked and re-set to these gaps whenever removed, to insure easy starting. Always carry a spare plug well protected, for emergency use on the line.

Replacement spark plugs must be 18 millimeter size, and they should duplicate the factory plug closely. For best results use the F5730 plug. Don't use plugs with long bodies or points which project into the engine further than the original. Such plugs overheat and cause preignition, and the piston may strike them.

TIMER

Keep timer connections clean and tight, and the contact points free from grit and oil. The timer must be adjusted closely on the side bearing, yet it must be free to move when the spark is "advanced" or "retarded."

Best ignition is obtained with the contact points adjusted from .020" to .025" opening. Following is an easy way to set them:—turn flywheels so the wiping block clears timer blade, then loosen locknut on timer adjusting screw PB-17G. Turn this screw down until the two points just touch, then back screw out a full ½ turn and tighten the locknut. This gives .020" to .025" opening.

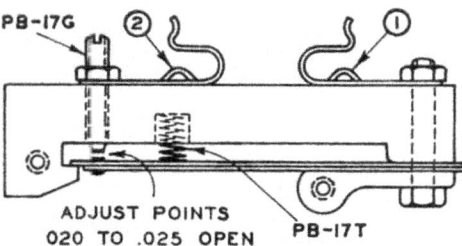

If the points burn or wear unevenly, dress them with a fine file, pocket stone, or fine emery cloth. Be sure they match and seat together evenly when adjusted.

When the wiping block wears, loosen the bolt in flywheel hub and turn the block to a new wearing position, then tighten bolt snugly.

To renew a timer blade remove PB-17P screw which clamps the timer fiber and the ground block together.

Loosen upper mounting screw, then swing fiber clear to permit access to all parts (see cut). Be careful not to lose the PB-17T spiral spring. Re-check all adjustments after assembly.

The "arc of contact" or interval during which the timer contact points close the electrical circuit to produce the spark, should be approximately 30 degrees to 35 degrees or $\frac{1}{12}$ a crankshaft revolution. This measures 5" to 5½" on the flywheel circumference. The "arc of contact" can be re-set if necessary, by loosening the top mounting screw which holds the timer fiber block, and shifting this block closer to, or further from the flywheel hub. Don't change the contact point screw adjustment to set the "arc of contact."

CARBURETOR

Use only genuine FAIRMONT gaskets to repair carburetors. They can be used over many times whereas paper and makeshift gaskets seldom fit and they tear easily and leak. Never use thick gaskets, for they do not allow parts to assemble together properly.

The carburetor is designed with a vertical check valve to prevent troubles common to horizontal check valves used on two-cycle engines. Springs on the check valve and air valve are set with correct tension at the factory and they should not be changed.

The carburetor control knob on the car housing, turns to open or close the needle valve, and pulls up to choke the carburetor. If needle valve is opened too far, the mixture contains too much gasoline, and will be "rich." The engine will then miss explosions, lack power and waste fuel. Black smoke from the exhaust indicates a "rich" mixture.

With needle valve closed too much there is not enough gasoline in the mixture and it is "lean." A "lean" mixture will not fire easily, and it gives a weak explosion, even when spark is advanced. It also causes engine to run unevenly, missing a few explosions or back firing, then firing a few times before missing again.

The needle valve should always be set so the engine runs best with the least gasoline. The best adjustment for a warm engine is between ¾ and 1 turn opening of needle valve.

When starting engine in cold weather, needle valve should be opened at least a turn more than the regular adjustment, and choke also used. After engine is running and warmed up needle valve can be closed to the regular adjustment. When running fast or pulling heavy loads, it is necessary to close needle valve slightly more than when running light. Don't close needle valve when stopping engine. Never screw it shut hard—this ruins the fine pointed end and makes carburetor hard to adjust.

Sometimes a hot engine will start hard after standing a short time. This is caused by "flooding," or a very rich mixture forming in the crankcase. A "flooded" engine can be cleaned out by opening crankcase drain cock and rocking flywheels to blow out the rich mixture.

The small vent hole in body of carburetor must be kept open. If gasoline runs out of vent, or constantly drips from carburetor, float valve is not seating properly. To remedy this trouble first take off and clean strainer bowl and drain carburetor. Then rotate float valve, pressing down on it at same time to make it seat. This will dislodge particles that may be the cause of flooding.

If float valve continues to leak shut off gasoline, remove carburetor bowl, and inspect float valve, float lever bearing and hinge pin. New parts should be applied if these are badly worn, screws holding float to lever should be tightened, and float level should be checked. To tightly seat a new float valve assemble it in the bowl with the guide. Lightly tap the end of the valve, turning it several times and finally rotate it against the seat with pressure to burnish the surfaces.

With cork float lifted to its high position and float valve tight on the seat, the top surface of float should be ⅜ to 7/16 inch below top rim of bowl. The float lever can be carefully bent if it is necessary to change the float level. Be sure to check the float level whenever the carburetor bowl is removed, and replace all gaskets when assembling.

The carburetor strainer bowl should be taken off and cleaned regularly as instructed under "Fuel System." Give carburetor an occasional cleaning and tighten all screws and nuts. Never wipe with rags or wastte when engine is running as litt may be drawn in and thus cause trouble.

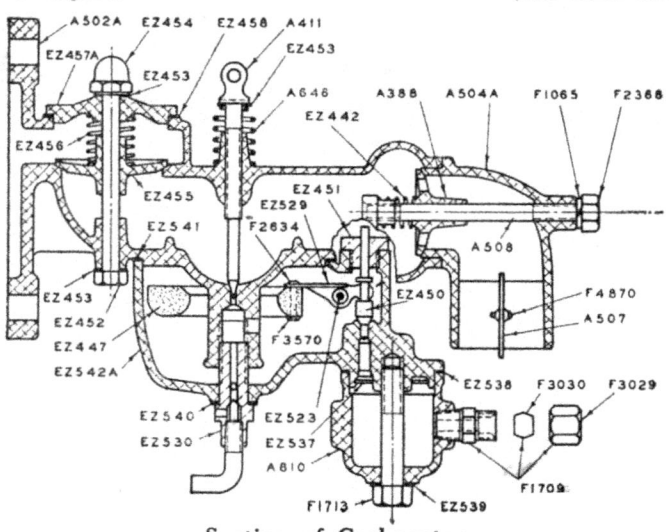

Section of Carburetor

PISTON AND CONNECTING ROD

Aluminum alloy pistons and connecting rods are softer than like parts of iron and steel and they must be handled with more care. Don't drop them or clamp tightly in vises as they may spring out of shape.

Cast iron pistons should never be used with aluminum connecting rods, nor steel connecting rods with aluminum pistons, for there is wide difference in the weights of the two groups

Bulletin 294A—Page 19
Fairmont M19 Car—Series C

and an engine would be thrown out of balance.

Under no circumstances should a cast iron piston and steel connecting rod be installed in place of the aluminum parts, for high compression would cause overheating, preignition and knocking.

Piston pins on early engines were fitted tight, by heating the pistons in boiling water and inserting the pins cold. With late improvements in aluminum alloys and newer methods of finishing the parts to close dimensions, Aluminum Co. of America engineers now recommend looser fitting as explained following, and old instructions are void.

ALUMINUM ALLOY CONNECTING ROD

Aluminum alloy connecting rods are drop forged and heat treated for strength, before machining. Care must be used not to spring them, for even though straightened again they may go out of shape thereafter, and misalignment then results.

The bronze piston pin bushing is pressed in the connecting rod and afterward bored and reamed for .001" clearance on the hardened piston pin, to insure correct fit and alignment. These parts seldom require replacement, but when the old rod does wear it should be exchanged complete for a new one as explained in the next paragraph.

Bearing metal is spun in the crankpin end and broached to size, thereby securing a dense wear resisting bearing. Rebabbitting in the field is not practical, but connecting rods in perfect condition except for worn bearings, can be exchanged for new ones at a nominal charge. Write for details.

Because of the light reciprocating weight of the piston and connecting rod, there is little wear on the connecting rod bearings, and adjustment is seldom required. If after long service this bearing does wear until it pounds or knocks, it should be taken up. A dull rattling sound in the crankcase as an engine slows down usually indicates a worn or loose connecting rod bearing.

The connecting rod must be fitted .002" to .003" loose on the crankpin to provide proper clearance for lubrication. To reach the connecting rod, first shut off fuel and take off carburetor. Remove lock wire and cap screws from connecting rod, and carefully lift off the cap and shims. Peel off one or more thin layers from each shim, according to the amount of looseness to be taken up.

Before replacing the parts, lay a 1¼" square piece of .003" paper or shim stock between the cap and crankpin, then carefully reassemble exactly as removed. When the two cap screws are tightly drawn to place, the bearing should be a snug (not tight) fit, permitting the engine to turn freely. If the bearing is still too loose, peel another layer from each shim and test again. After proper adjustment is secured, remove the test shim, reassemble tight, and lock cap screws with wire.

NOTE—Early engines had connecting rods without shims, and the caps must be carefully filed to make adjustment for wear.

ALUMINUM ALLOY PISTON

Aluminum alloy pistons are accurately ground from heat treated castings made in permanent molds. This insures uniform thickness and expansion, and minimum weight. As aluminum expands more than cast iron when heated, pistons must be fitted in the cylinders with .008" to .010" clearance at the skirt end, at normal temperatures. This insures their fitting the cylinders without binding when engines are heated in operation.

When starting a cold engine the piston is sometimes noisy because of excessive clearance. Always idle the engine slowly for several minutes to warm up and expand the piston and cylinder evenly. Never operate with open throttle until warmed up, for the piston will expand faster than the cylinder and these parts are liable to seize and score.

To pull piston from cylinder, first shut off fuel and remove carburetor, then disconnect connecting rod as instructed in preceding section. Drain water jacket, remove cylinder head, and scrape carbon from cylinder walls after which piston and connecting rod can be pulled. When replacing piston be sure the deflector is in proper position (see cut on page 15). If piston is put in upside down the engine will start hard and lack power.

Narrow rings are used on aluminum pistons to prevent drag on the cylinder walls, and rapid wear in the grooves. The rings have no dowels, and they must be free in the grooves so they can expand and properly seal the cylinder and steady the piston in the bore. Stuck or broken rings are sometimes responsible for a noisy piston. Always replace rings with genuine

FAIRMONT rings having the interlocking joint, for ordinary step or diagonal cut rings catch in the ports. As heavy oils carbonize quickly and stick the rings it is important to use proper oil as explained on page 6.

The piston pin, and holes into which it fits in the piston and connecting rod, are finished to very close dimensions to insure proper assembly without fitting. At normal temperatures the pin should push tight into the piston by hand and the connecting rod should rock freely on it. Lock rings prevent the pin from working out of the piston. The holes in the piston must not be enlarged by reaming, as the pin would fit too loose after the parts became heated. Always order the A853 piston with rings, piston pin, and lock rings when a replacement piston is needed, so as to have a proper fitting assembly of parts.

After assembling a piston pin and applying lock rings, measure the diameter of the piston in several places to be sure it is round. Careful caliper measurements will suffice but a micrometer is better. If found out of shape lightly tap it with a soft mallet or wood block to bring it back round and true.

Aluminum pistons seldom require replacement until worn .006" to .008" looser in the bore, than originally fitted. A worn piston which is noisy when cold, or even after warmed up, may still be good for long service if there is no objection to slight noise while operating the car. Replacement in such cases must be decided by the operator or repairman. Often a noisy piston can be quieted by pulling it from the cylinder, and carefully tapping the sides with a soft mallet or block of wood until slightly out of round, with the vertical dimension a few thousandths larger than the horizontal one.

FLYWHEELS

Flywheels are properly located on the crankshaft tapers by hardened keys, and tightly drawn to place by nuts. Don't try to drive flywheels off as spokes are liable to be cracked, the crankshaft sprung, or ball bearings damaged.

To remove a flywheel, first pull cotter and unscrew crankshaft nut. On the belt side also drive out pin which engages starting crank. With a brass or lead hammer weighing about 3 lbs. sharply strike the end of crankshaft, at the same time pulling outward on the flywheel rim. Flywheels which have been in place a long time may stick, in which case a jaw wheel puller should be used to remove them.

When replacing a flywheel wipe all parts clean and oil well, then draw crankshaft nut fairly tight and insert cotter. If a new key, flywheel, or crankshaft is used in assembly be sure the key fits freely in the keyway, and the flywheel keyway does not bind on top of the key, otherwise flywheel will not go to proper place on the taper.

NOTE—Engines No. 45367 and higher use belt flywheel A706 and crankshaft A711, while earlier ones require belt flywheel A537 and crankshaft A527. The tapers are differently located in these two groups of parts, with respect to the engine pulley, hence they should not be interchanged separately. When a belt flywheel or crankshaft is required for engines below No. 45367, A706 and A711 should be ordered together.

BALL BEARINGS

Ball bearing installations on FAIRMONT equipment have been thoroughly tested and approved by the ball bearing manufacturers' engineers. The bearings themselves must have proper load capacities and clearances to insure satisfactory service.

Many ball bearings which appear to be exactly like the approved ones installed at the factory, are designed for light loads and they do not stand up when used as substitutes. For the same reason "reground" bearings do not stand up in this service.

Use only genuine new ball bearings made to highest standards and as approved for FAIRMONT equipment when replacements become necessary.

Don't strike ball bearings with steel hammers. Always drive them off evenly with a brass punch and strike against the inner races only, being careful not to spring or damage the ball retainers. A piece of clean tubing which just slips over the shaft is best to drive them back in place.

Never lay bearings on work benches where grit and metal particles will get in the races, and don't use torches to heat bearings when removing them, for the hardened balls and races will be ruined.

Wash in clean gasoline or hot soda bath as soon as removed. Don't use dirty gasoline or bath containing grit and metal particles, for once such foreign matter lodges in the races it cannot be thoroughly washed out.

As soon as a bearing is washed lubricate it with clean oil, and wrap in

CRANKSHAFT AND BALL BEARINGS

Before doing any work on the crankshaft or ball bearings, carefully read the preceding section, "Ball Bearings."

The crankshaft and ball bearings are lubricated by oil which enters the crankcase mixed in the fuel. The outboard ball bearing next to the belt flywheel is packed with high grade acid free semi-fluid lubricant when assembled at the factory, and in service it receives a seepage of oil through the side bearing packing. Surplus lubricant sometimes oozes from this bearing on a new engine, but soon works itself out. Once a month remove the pipe plug in the belt side bearing casting and add a small quantity of clean oil to the outboard ball bearing, being careful no foreign matter enters.

If necessary to remove crankshaft, first disconnect connecting rod, (see page 19) then push piston and connecting rod assembly back in the cylinder. Next take off flywheels (see page 20).

Remove four nuts holding belt side bearing casting and carefully drive it off with outer ball bearing, using a block of wood. Remove timer side bearing casting the same way and unscrew two side bearing studs from top of crankcase on timer side.

Turn crankpin straight down in crankcase. Carefully lift out the crankshaft from the timer side of crankcase, working it upward so ball bearing clears the place where studs were removed. Do not use force. Two ball bearings are pressed on the crankshaft. If necessary to remove them drive off evenly with a brass punch against inner races only.

Next remove cover from belt side bearing casting and jar out the outboard ball bearing, bearing washer, and packing sleeve. Wash clean and immediately oil and protect the bearing.

Before reassembling, smooth burrs and rough places on the crankshaft shoulders and fillets, then carefully drive the bearings to place until they "seat" against the shoulders. Be sure the "loading grooves" or notches in the bearing races, face away from the crankshaft shoulders.

Clean crankcase gasket joints, and oil ball bearings before reassembling the crankshaft in reverse order from the way it was removed. Screw in side bearing studs, apply a new gasket, and start the timer side bearing casting on the ball bearing squarely, then carefully drive to place.

When applying side bearing nuts first draw one up just snug, then draw the opposite one an equal amount. Set the remaining two the same way and finally tighten all four nuts evenly so as not to distort the casting or break the lugs.

Next "seat" the ball bearing to place in the timer side bearing casting by light blows on the opposite end of the crankshaft. Then apply the belt side bearing casting with a new gasket, having pipe plug up, and tighten as instructed for timer side. Be sure this side bearing is drawn evenly to place and concentric with the crankshaft, so as not to throw the outboard ball bearing out of alignment.

NOTE—Side bearing castings fit very closely on the ball bearings and they must be driven to place carefully.

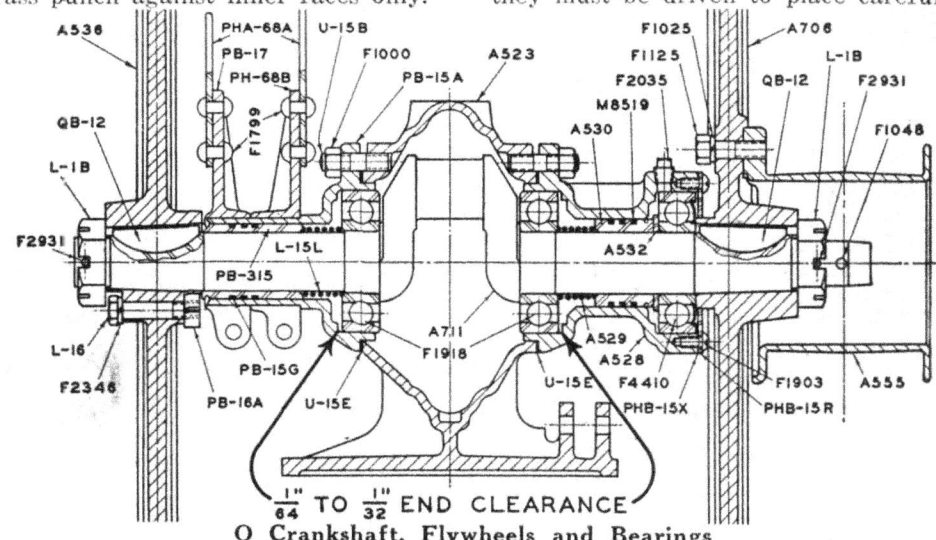

$\frac{1}{64}$ TO $\frac{1}{32}$ END CLEARANCE

O Crankshaft, Flywheels and Bearings

Heating the side bearings in boiling water and wiping dry, will insure of easier assembly.

The crankshaft and ball bearing assembly must have $\frac{1}{64}"$ to $\frac{1}{32}"$ end clearance when side bearing castings are bolted in place. (See cut.) Check this by carefully striking the crankshaft on one end, then on the other, and measure to note the amount it shifts. An extra gasket may have to be added at one or both side bearings, to secure clearance. Be sure there is end play in the assembly so ball bearings are not pinched and overloaded.

On the belt side insert the spring and packing sleeve with rings, being careful not to break rings. This sleeve can be held in place against spring pressure by a screw driver slipped through the pipe plug hole in side bearing casting.

Pack the outboard bearing with clean semi-fluid lubricant, then slip bearing washer over crankshaft and install the bearing with shielded side out. Drive it in flush with the side bearing face, apply cover with gasket, and screw in pipe plug.

After installing spring and packing on the timer side, flywheels and remaining parts can be reassembled.

RINGSEALD PACKING

Each side bearing is sealed against crankcase compression by Ringseald packing. This consists of three compression rings carried by a grooved sleeve closely fitting the crankshaft. Coil springs hold these sleeves in proper position and prevent their turning on the crankshaft.

The compression rings expand in the side bearing castings and remain stationary, while the sleeves rotate with the crankshaft. The parts are lubricated from the crankcase and provide an effective seal. Unless damaged the parts will wear indefinitely.

If packing leaks badly when an engine is running, rings may be broken or parts badly roughened. Slight leakage is sometimes noticeable when turning an engine slowly by hand, but this disappears when running. Condensation of low grade fuel inside a cold engine may cause seepage through the packing but as soon as the engine warms up this disappears.

The packing sleeve and rings can easily be removed from the timer side of the engine after taking off the flywheel. The belt side bearing must be removed from the crankcase to get at packing on that side.

When fitting new packing rings they must be free in the grooves and the gaps should have about .003" opening.

THROTTLE

The throttle valve is a specially shaped tapered sleeve fitting in a tapered hole over the intake ports. Movement of the throttle lever rocks this valve varying the volume of fresh gas entering the cylinder and thereby controls the power of the engine. The design of this valve insures fresh gas reaching the spark plug, even when the throttle is nearly closed.

Leakage at the throttle stem is prevented by a felt packing inside a steel cup. The stop screw in the opposite cover controls the amount of valve travel. The throttle arm is held in place by a clamp screw which must be kept tight. If this arm slips the throttle valve may not open properly.

The throttle valve can be pulled out from the belt side of the engine after removing flywheel and valve cover.

CARBON DEPOSITS

After an engine has seen long service the piston head, inside of cylinder head, and walls of the combustion chamber become coated with carbon. Knocking or "pinging," with overheating and loss of power then occur when the engine is warmed up, especially when pulling loads. Carbon can be carefully scraped out after draining water and removing the cylinder head.

Badly carbonized intake and exhaust ports cause an engine to start hard and lack power, therefore they should also be cleaned while the head is off. The throttle valve and muffler can be removed to get at the ports if necessary. Wipe or blow out all loose carbon before reassembling.

Carbon sometimes also accumulates inside of the piston head and deflector. These deposits must be cleaned out so fresh gases entering the crankcase can cool the piston head.

When replacing cylinder head be sure the gasket and joints are clean. First tighten every other cylinder head nut just snug, then set the remainder the same way. Next go over all of them, tightening to place evenly. After the engine has been run until heated up, tighten them once more.

Excessive quantities of oil mixed in the gasoline, or poor oil, result in heavy carbon deposits. Be sure to follow oil recommendations and mixing instructions on pages 5 and 6.

Bulletin 294A—Page 23
Fairmont M19 Car—Series C

EXTRA EQUIPMENT

The following extra equipment can be furnished for the FAIRMONT M19 Series C motor car:

WIDE WINDSHIELD M16412
LEFT SIDE SEAT M16298
RIGHT SIDE SEAT M16314

Similar to Standard windshield except wider to shelter projecting side seat shown.

Side seats, both back and seat are well padded and placed in the most comfortable position for efficient track inspection.

STANDARD WINDSHIELD M15984

Easily applied in field, or removed and folded for carrying on car.

Heavy celluloid window. Khaki colored duck-to-drill with inner layer of gum rubber.

CANVAS COVER M7951

Good investment if car is left standing outside. No. 10 brown duck, 7x9 feet, fire proofed with "Preservo." Eyelets for tying.

SEAT CUSHION F4871

Java Kapok fiber covered with brown Dupont Fabrikoid. Straps hold cushion in place. Size 13x16½x2″, not illustrated.

DRY CELL HEADLIGHT M8404

Adjustable from narrow 300-foot beam to wide spreading light for close work. Two 6″ dry cells give 7 to 8 hours continuous light or last months if used intermittently. 4¾″ silvered reflector; aluminum case; car bracket included. Safe to use around gasoline.

RAIL SWEEPS M15171

Clear rails of stones or obstructions liable to derail car. Discarded air hose is held ahead of front wheels by spring hinged arms which raise automatically when car is set off. Hose not included.

10-INCH GONG M16417

Good and loud. Durable clapper operated by pull wire on seat. Mounted out of way of load and passengers. Widely used as warning signal.

6-INCH GONG M9005

Provides warning signal if required, at minimum cost.

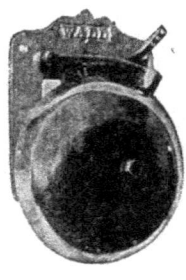

HIGH TENSION MAGNETO

Choice of Robert Bosch, Eisemann or Wico. Improved long life ball bearing drive. Write for information if interested and give engine number. Can be furnished on new cars or applied to old ones.

AIR HORN M17331

Three trumpets with pleasing tones give a warning signal which carries long distances. A quick pull on the rod operates it. No batteries, no valves, nothing to wear.

MUFFLER M17308

Riders desiring exceptionally quiet operation will be pleased with this muffler, which was released only after long research and thorough testing on track. The power loss is very small. Not illustrated.

Bulletin 294A—Page 25
Fairmont M19 Car—Series C

INSTRUCTIONS FOR ORDERING PARTS

When this bulletin is received complete the following motor car record from the FAIRMONT name plates on the car, and on the engine water jacket. The engine number is also stamped on top of the crankcase. Always mention these factory serial numbers when writing about the car or ordering parts. Don't give us railroad numbers.

Factory Car No.................................... Car Class ....

Factory Engine No.................Engine Type................Engine H. P...........

TO INSURE PROMPT AND CORRECT SHIPMENT of parts on order always give:

      (1)   Quantity of each part wanted.
      (2)   Symbol number of part as shown in this book.
      (3)   Description of part as shown in this book.
      (4)   Factory serial numbers recorded above.
      (5)   Car gauge if other than 56½" standard.
      (6)   State whether shipment is to be by mail, express, or freight.

All parts are shipped f. o. b. factory, transportation charges to be paid by customer. Terms are strictly cash with order.

Parts are listed by description, symbol, and quantity, and all important items illustrated. Quantities in right hand columns show the number of parts in each assembly or group.

Items printed in capitals are assemblies which include all parts listed immediately following and indented to the right. When assemblies can be used, always order them to save work of fitting separate parts.

When symbol is known, consult the index on pages 26 and 27 to locate standard parts or determine their weights. If car is magneto equipped see bulletin 202 for magneto parts. If in doubt as to any part wanted, send full description or sketch, or send old part with order.

Bolts, nuts, washers, etc., are listed following the parts with which they are used. A complete list of them by size is also given on page 52.

CAR IDENTIFICATION

Standard cars are classed as M19 Series C when battery equipped, and as MM19 Series C when magneto equipped. When these cars have changes made from standard for customers they become special, and the designations are followed by figures.

For example the M19 Series C is known as M19 Series C4 when fitted with 14" torpedo proof wheels, the MM19 Series C becomes MM19 Series C11 when fitted with 14" torpedo proof wheels and certain housing parts of aluminum.

As printed, this bulletin covers standard Series C cars only but most of the parts illustrated and listed also fit the cars having special designations. When this bulletin is supplied for one of the special cars, a supplement accompanies it showing the special items or else their symbols are marked in the printed parts section.

If no supplement or marked bulletin is available, select special parts by illustration and printed symbol from the standard list as explained above and give serial numbers and car designation so proper material can be furnished from factory.

Page 26—Bulletin 294A
Fairmont M19 Car—Series C

WEIGHT AND NUMERICAL PART INDEX

Symbol	Weight (Approx)	Page
L-1B	5 oz.	31
PN-8A	2 oz.	29
QB-12	2 oz.	31
PB-15A	2 lbs.	31
PHM-15B	2 oz.	39
U-15B	1 oz.	29, 31
U-15E	¼ oz.	31
PB-15G	½ oz.	31-39
L-15L	3 oz.	31
PHB-15R	6 oz.	31
PHB-15X	¼ oz.	31
L-16	3 oz.	35
PB-16A	1 oz.	35
PB-17	10 oz.	35
PB-17G	1 oz.	35
PB-17P	½ oz.	35
QB-17P	½ oz.	35
PB-17T	½ oz.	35
PH-20	5 oz.	29
Q-21	5 oz.	29
QH-21A	3 oz.	29
P-21D	½ oz.	29
QB-21E	2 oz.	29
QB-21F	1 oz.	29
D-47D	1 oz.	29, 33
C-48	½ oz.	37
PHM-56C	3 oz.	39
PHM-56D	5 oz.	39
PHM-56H	1 oz.	38
PHM-58F	10 oz.	39
PHM-58G	2 oz.	39
PHM-58H	8 oz.	39
PHM-58L	1 oz.	39
PHM-58O	¼ oz.	39
D-65B	2 oz.	29
P-65B	1 oz.	41
PHA-68A	6½ oz.	35
PH-68B	10½ oz.	35
PHM-68B	10 oz.	35
PHA-68G	1 oz.	35
TF-68E	2 oz.	29
PH-90F	½ oz.	32
PHM-256	9 oz.	39
QHM-258	8 oz.	39
PHA-268	1 lb.	35
PHMA-268	1 lb.	35
TF-268-2	3 oz.	29
PH-293	6 oz.	38
LM-315	4 oz.	39
PB-315	8 oz.	31
A355	1¼ lbs.	35
A388	¼ oz.	33
F400	1 lb.	37
F401	½ oz.	37
F402	2½ oz.	37
F403	6 oz.	37
F404	1 oz.	37
F405	1 oz.	37
A406	1 oz.	29
A411	1½ oz.	33
A426	¼ oz.	39
EZ442	¼ oz.	33
EZ447	¼ oz.	33
EZ450	¼ oz.	33
EZ451	½ oz.	33
EZ452	1 oz.	33
EZ453	¼ oz.	33
EZ454	¼ oz.	33
B455	½ oz.	29
EZ455	1 oz.	33
EZ456	¼ oz.	33
EZ457A	1 oz.	33
EZ458	¼ oz.	33
EZ492	¼ oz.	33
A502A	1 lb.	33
A503A	5 oz.	33
A504A	3 oz.	33
A505	1 oz.	33
A507	1 oz.	33
A508	1 oz.	33
EZ515	½ oz.	33
A522	39 lbs.	29
A523	36 lbs.	29
EZ523	½ oz.	33
A524	1½ oz.	29
A526	10 lbs.	31
EZ526	¼ oz.	33
A527	8 lbs.	31
A528	3½ lbs.	31
EZ528	2 oz.	33
A529	1 oz.	31
EZ529	¼ oz.	33
A530	7 oz.	31
EZ530	1 oz.	33
A532	1 oz.	31
A534	¼ oz.	29
A535	5 oz.	29
A536	21½ lbs.	31
A537	21½ lbs.	31
EZ537	¼ oz.	33
A538	3 lbs.	28
EZ538	¼ oz.	33
A539	1½ lbs.	28
EZ539	¼ oz.	33
A540	1¼ lbs.	28
EZ540	¼ oz.	33
A541	1 lb.	28
EZ541	¼ oz.	33
EZ542A	6 oz.	33
A544	½ oz.	28
A545	1 oz.	28
A546	6 oz.	28
A547	1 oz.	28
A548	1½ oz.	29
A549	4½ lbs.	29
A550	7½ lbs.	29
A551	7¼ lbs.	29
A554	1 oz.	29
A555	3½ lbs.	41
A557	⅛ oz.	29
A593	3 oz.	35
A594	1½ oz.	35
A595	¼ oz.	35
A598	1 oz.	35
A607	½ oz.	39
A638	8 oz.	29
A642	2½ lbs.	33
A646	¼ oz.	33
A662	1 lb.	35
A706	22 lbs.	31
A707	1 oz.	39
A711	8 lbs.	31
A712	10 lbs.	31
A719	3 oz.	39
A726	12 oz.	39
A731	¼ oz.	38
A732	6 oz.	38
A764	37 lbs.	29
A765	41 lbs.	29
A794	¼ oz.	39
A795	12 oz.	39
A798	7 oz.	39
A799	¼ oz.	39
A800	6 oz.	39
A801	¼ oz.	39
A803	7 lbs.	39
A804	5 lbs.	39
A805	8 oz.	39
A806	4 oz.	39
A807	7 oz.	39
A810	2 oz.	33
A847	9 oz.	39
A853	2 lbs.	28
A860	2 lbs.	28
A864	6 oz.	38
F1022	2 oz.	29
F1023	5 oz.	29
F1081	2 lbs.	37
F1331	½ oz.	29
F1402	¾ oz. pr ft.	37
F1421	1½ oz.	37
F1615	1½ oz.	43
1696	1 oz.	47
F1709	½ oz.	32-33
F1741	2 oz.	29
F1854	1½ oz.	29
F1918	1 lb.	31
M2314	¼ oz.	37
F2551	¼ oz.	39
F2556	½ oz.	39
F2616	1 lb.	45
F2625	5 oz. pr ft.	29
F2666	½ oz.	29
F2676	¼ oz.	39
F2691	3½ oz.	29
F2707	4 oz.	43
F2754	½ oz.	43
F2764	4 oz.	32
F2945	12 oz.	37
F2946	8 oz.	37
F2947	14 oz.	37
F2948	2 oz.	37
F2950	2 oz.	37
F2951	5 oz.	37
F2952	10 oz.	37
F2958	¼ oz. pr ft.	37
F2966	3 oz.	37
F3000	1¼ lbs.	41
F3002	5 oz.	41
F3006	¾ oz. pr ft.	29
F3007	½ oz.	51
F3029	¼ oz.	32
F3030	¼ oz.	32
F3032	¼ oz.	39
F3039	¼ oz.	51
F3054	½ oz.	28-35-41
F3271	6½ lbs.	38
F3300	½ oz.	37
F3301	2 oz.	29

Bulletin 294A—Page 26A
Fairmont M19 Car—Series C

ESTIMATING PRICE LIST

This list covers all parts shown in M19 Series C car bulletin 294A effective December 1st, 1935.

The prices are for estimating purposes only in the United States. They are issued for convenience in preparing requisitions and estimating repair costs.

A reasonable amount has been added to these prices to cover transportation, so that they can be considered as approximate costs of the parts f. o. b. destination in the United States.

Part	Price	Part	Price	Part	Price	Part	Price
L-1B	.35	A355	5.45	A538	19.25	A810	1.35
PN-8A	.10	A388	.75	EZ538	.04	A847	4.95
QB-12	.25	F400	.45	A539	8.90	A853	9.15
PB-15A	3.30	F401	.45	EZ539	.03	A860	7.80
PHM-15B	.10	F402	1.40	A540	6.90	A864	1.50
U-15B	.05	F403	2.20	EZ540	.04	F1022	.45
U-15E	.04	F404	1.65	A541	9.35	F1023	.90
PB-15G	.18	F405	1.10	EZ541	.05	F1081	.50
L-15L	.30	A406	.50	EZ542A	2.75	F1331	.03
PHB-15R	.45	A411	.50	A544	.10	F1402 per ft.	.20
PHB-15X	.05	A426	.25	A545	.25	F1421	.25
L-16	.20	EZ442	.25	A546	.70	F1615	.02
PB-16A	.35	EZ447	.70	A547	.10	1696	.15
PB-17	.85	EZ450	.45	A548	.55	F1709	.20
PB-17G	.30	EZ451	.25	A549	3.00	F1741	1.05
PB-17P	.20	EZ452	.75	A550	15.60	F1854	.20
QB-17P	.20	EZ453	.03	A551	11.00	F1918	3.90
PB-17T	.05	EZ454	.20	A554	.15	M2314	.15
PH-20	2.75	B455	.10	A555	5.35	F2551	.01
Q-21	1.05	EZ455	.95	A557	.15	F2556	.30
QH-21A	.80	EZ456	.25	A593	3.85	F2616	2.75
P-21D	.05	EZ457A	.90	A594	1.65	F2625 per ft.	.35
QB-21E	.30	EZ458	.04	A595	.70	F2666	.05
QB-21F	.15	EZ492	.15	A598	.55	F2676	.10
D-47D	.15	A502A	7.55	A607	.10	F2691	.15
C-48	.15	A503A	4.40	A638	1.45	F2707	.07
PHM-56C	2.00	A504A	1.50	A642	15.40	F2754	7.00
PHM-56D	.85	A505	.90	A646	.10	F2764	.85
PHM-56H	.85	A507	.15	A662	1.15	F2945	.25
PHM-58F	2.50	A508	.75	A706	6.60	F2946	.45
PHM-58G	.50	EZ515	.15	A707	.03	F2947	.55
PHM-58H	2.30	A522	36.00	A711	21.50	F2948	.25
PHM-58L	5.50	A523	27.50	A712	29.25	F2950	.45
PHM-58D	.02	EZ523	.20	A719	3.00	F2951	.55
D-65B	.05	A524	.15	A726	1.00	F2952	.65
P-65B	.10	A526	31.30	A731	.17	F2958 per ft.	.05
PHA-68A	.35	EZ526	.05	A732	2.15	F2966	.30
PH-68B	.90	A527	21.50	A764	30.15	F3000	3.30
PHM-68B	.96	A528	6.40	A765	38.40	F3002	1.40
PHA-68G	.35	EZ528	.80	A794	.08	F3006 per ft.	.20
TF-68E	.40	A529	.25	A795	7.25	F3007	.30
PH-90F	.20	EZ529	.15	A798	1.45	F3009	6.90
PHM-256	3.50	A530	2.15	A799	.03	F3030	.03
QHM-258	3.35	EZ530	.40	A800	1.00	F3032	.15
PHA-268	1.90	A532	.25	A801	.03	F3039	.15
PHMA-268	1.90	A534	.15	A803	18.70	F3054 per ft.	.05
TF-268-2	.50	A535	2.00	A804	7.70	F3271	35.75
PH-293	2.00	A536	7.70	A805	2.20	F3300	.65
LM-315	1.50	A537	6.60	A806	1.25	F3301	.55
PB-315	2.00	EZ537	.15	A807	4.30	F3357	.03

(continued on other side of sheet)

Fairmont M19 Car—Series C

Part	Price	Part	Price	Part	Price	Part	Price
F3596	.25	M6572	1.80	M13545	3.30	M15983	1.40
F3607	.35	M6574	1.05	M13550	.30	M15984	8.80
F3613	.55	M6575	.70	M13551	.30	M15985	7.10
F3614	.35	M6577	.10	M13552	4.00	M16031	.50
F3620	4.10	M6582	1.20	M13553	4.15	M16054	.55
F3639	4.00	M6592	3.10	M13556	1.90	M16224	1.05
F3651	.25	M6594	1.10	M13557	.95	M16298	10.50
F3741	.45	M6596	2.00	M13558	3.55	M16314	10.50
F3853	.08	M6715	1.75	M13562	4.00	M16354	3.30
F3854	.25	M6738	.12	M13563	3.30	M16411	.90
F3855	.08	M6880	.70	M13564	2.75	M16412	10.50
F4166	.55	M6992	.20	M13566	.70	M16413	8.00
F4179	2.00	M6993	.30	M13567	3.85	M16414	1.00
F4180	1.10	M6994	.30	M13568	.30	M16415	.50
F4200	.30	M7013	1.40	M13569	7.30	M16417	7.70
F4231 per ft.	.45	M7016	.20	M13570	9.70	M16420	4.00
F4410	4.20	M7021	.05	M13571	4.25	M16432	2.10
F4413	.40	M7032	1.90	M13581	.40	M16489	1.40
F4734	.05	M7035	2.00	M13595	.25	M16490	4.15
F4756	4.30	M7036	.30	M13610	2.15	M16491	.50
F4757	1.15	M7157	.45	M13666	1.05	M16492	.50
F4761	.06	M7187	.05	M13670	.40	M16493	.30
F4870	.03	M7256	.70	M14232	.80	M16495	.17
F4871	3.85	M7281	.35	M14238	.90	M16496	.65
F4937	17.60	M7285	.30	M14257	1.40	M16642	.25
F4938	1.15	M7289	.25	M14650	.90	M16675	3.85
M5027	.15	M7290	1.10	M14700	.90	M17112	.20
M5053	.55	M7469	.15	M14702	1.00	M17308	9.90
M5058	.25	M7503	.25	M14886	2.75	M17331	18.50
M5073	.80	M7666	13.75	M14924	.35	M18413	3.50
M5106	.55	M7951	16.85	M14940	1.55	M18801	.15
F5115	.70	M8403	1.10	M14949	1.35	M18930	.40
F5168	.50	M8404	12.50	M14950	.65	M18931	.20
F5324	26.95	M8519	.30	M14980	.30	M18963	1.35
M5445	.10	M8520	2.90	M14981	.45	M19104	1.10
F5730	.70	M8697	1.05	M14987	.50	M19105	.45
M6001	.05	M8705	1.66	M14988	1.50	M19402	9.10
M6023	5.80	M8742	5.75	M14990	.60	M19403	.40
M6334	.65	M9005	3.95	M15066	3.85	M19405	9.70
M6426	1.60	M9207	.30	M15068	.30	M19406	.45
M6427	.80	M9210	.15	M15069	.30	M19407	3.30
M6428	1.00	M9214	.25	M15070	.20	M19409	3.30
M6429	.20	M9245	.20	M15083	1.05	M19412	1.65
M6430	.70	M9877	.20	M15084	1.05	M19413	1.65
M6436	.95	M13461	.60	M15085	.45	M19835	1.05
M6438	.80	M13524	9.10	M15171	3.00	M19866	6.60
M6442	.45	M13525	6.00	M15183	.35	M19868	6.60
M6445	.30	M13527	.25	M15475	.20	M19874	.45
M6448	1.60	M13531	1.00	M15476	13.75	M20859A	3.85
M6472	.10	M13536	10.35	M15980	.55	M21138	2.20
M6540	.20	M13537	9.65	M15981	.80	M21273A	7.70
M6562	2.10	M13538	.35	M15982	.80	M21274A	3.85
M6566	.80						

Bulletin 294A—Page 27
Fairmont M19 Car—Series C

Part	Weight	Pg	Part	Weight	Pg	Part	Weight	Pg
F3357	½ oz.	43	M7021	4 oz.	51	M14981	2¾ oz.	47
F3596	1 oz.	43	M7032	3¼ lbs.	41	M14987	5 oz.	47
F3607	½ oz.	29	M7035	5½ lbs.	50	M14988	9 oz.	47
F3613	4 oz.	32	M7036	14 oz.	51	M14990	6 oz.	47
F3614	2 oz.	32	M7157	9 oz.	51	M15066	4 lbs.	32
F3620	1¼ lbs.	45	M7187	½ oz.	51	M15068	4 oz.	32
M3639	1 oz.	41	M7256	3 oz.	47	M15069	4 oz.	32
F3651	3 oz.	32	M7281	8¼ oz.	47	M15070	¾ oz.	32
F3741	13 oz.	37	M7285	3¼ oz.	47	M15083	3½ lbs.	51
F3853	¼ oz.	35	M7289	½ oz.	51	M15084	3¾ lbs.	51
F3854	1 oz.	35	M7290	1¾ lbs.	51	M15085	1 lb.	51
F3855	½ oz.	35	M7469	½ oz.	41	M15171	5½ lbs.	24
F4166	1 oz.	37	M7503	1½ oz.	41	M15183	2 oz.	47
F4179	1½ lbs.	37	M7666	3½ lbs.	43	M15475	1½ oz.	29
F4180	5 oz.	37	M7951	8 lbs.	23	M15476	10 lbs.	29
F4200	1 oz.	28	M8403	14 oz.	37	M15980	2¼ lbs.	47
F4231	8 oz. pr ft.	29	M8404	9 lbs.	37-24	M15981	6 oz.	47
F4410	1 lb.	31	M8519	1 oz.	31	M15982	6 oz.	47
F4413	7 oz.	37	M8520	2½ lbs.	51	M15983	8 oz.	47
F4734	⅓ oz.	28	M8697	1 lb.	43	M15984	11½ lbs.	47-23
F4756	2 lbs.	37	M8705	1½ lbs.	43	M15985	2½ lbs.	47
F4757	1 oz.	39	M8742	12½ lbs.	43	M16031	1½ lbs.	47
F4761	⅓ oz.	35	M9005	4 lbs.	24	M16054	4¼ lbs.	47
F4870	¼ oz.	33	M9207	1½ oz.	47	M16224	3 lbs.	51
F4871	2½ lbs.	24	M9210	½ oz.	47	M16298	18 lbs.	23
F4937	4½ lbs.	38	M9214	2 oz.	47	M16314	18 lbs.	23
F4938	4 oz.	38	M9245	¾ oz.	35	M16354	3 lbs.	37
M5027	2 oz.	45	M9877	1 oz.	35	M16411	7 oz.	47
M5053	5 oz.	41	M13464	1 lb.	41	M16412	12 lbs.	47-23
M5058	1 oz.	41	M13524	5¾ lbs.	45	M16413	3 lbs.	47
M5073	3 oz.	32	M13525	2½ lbs.	45	M16414	1½ lbs.	47
M5106	2½ oz.	51	M13527	2½ oz.	51	M16415	2 oz.	47
F5115	4 oz.	29	M13531	3¾ lbs.	49	M16417	9 lbs.	24
F5168	½ oz.	39	M13536	4½ lbs.	41	M16420	3½ lbs.	31
F5324	7 lbs.	38	M13537	4¼ lbs.	41	M16432	1¼ lbs.	47
M5445	1 oz.	32	M13538	6 oz.	49	M16489	3 lbs.	37
F5730	5 oz.	37	M13545	2½ lbs.	49	M16490	3¾ lbs.	37
M6001	½ oz.	43	M13550	1½ lbs.	49	M16491	1½ oz.	37
M6023	12½ lbs.	43	M13551	9 oz.	49	M16492	1 oz.	37
M6334	3 oz.	43	M13552	9 lbs.	49	M16493	2 oz.	37
M6426	3¼ lbs.	51	M13553	9 lbs.	49	M16495	3 oz.	37
M6427	1 lb.	51	M13556	6¼ lbs.	49	M16496	10 oz.	37
M6428	1¾ lbs.	51	M13557	4 lbs.	49	M16642	¼ oz.	37
M6429	10 oz.	51	M13558	6 lbs.	49	M16675	3½ lbs.	49
M6430	1 lb.	51	M13562	20½ lbs.	43	M17112	1 oz.	37
M6436	10 oz.	51	M13563	19 lbs.	43	M17308	4¾ lbs.	24
M6438	1 lb.	51	M13564	2¼ lbs.	45	M17331	5½ lbs.	24
M6442	8 oz.	51	M13566	4 oz.	45	M18413	25¾ lbs.	43
M6445	1 lb.	51	M13567	1¼ lbs.	45	M18801	1 oz.	45
M6448	4½ lbs.	50	M13568	1¼ lbs.	45	M18930	1 oz.	47
M6472	2 oz.	50	M13569	2¾ lbs.	45	M18931	¼ oz.	47
M6540	1½ oz.	51	M13570	6 lbs.	45	M18963	6 oz.	32
M6562	1½ lbs.	41	M13571	1¼ lbs.	45	M19104	1½ oz.	35
M6566	14 oz.	41	M13581	3¼ oz.	45	M19105	1 oz.	35
M6572	1½ lbs.	41	M13595	4 oz.	45	M19402	5¾ lbs.	45
M6574	8 oz.	41	M13610	5 lbs.	51	M19403	5 oz.	45
M6575	1½ lbs.	41	M13666	2¾ lbs.	51	M19405	6¼ lbs.	45
M6577	¾ oz.	41	M13670	2 oz.	35	M19406	1¼ oz.	49
M6582	3½ lbs.	41	M14232	1 lb.	47	M19407	7¾ lbs.	49
M6592	2¾ lbs.	51	M14238	4 lbs.	49	M19409	7¾ lbs.	49
M6594	2 lbs.	51	M14257	1¾ lbs.	51	M19412	4¾ lbs.	49
M6596	12 oz.	51	M14650	3 lbs.	47	M19413	4¾ lbs.	49
M6715	2¼ lbs.	49	M14700	3 lbs.	47	M19835	1 lb.	43
M6738	1 oz.	37	M14702	1¾ lbs.	47	M19866	38¼ lbs.	43
M6880	1½ oz.	43	M14886	2¼ lbs.	29-51	M19868	38¼ lbs.	43
M6992	6 oz.	51	M14924	4 oz.	47	M19874	9 oz.	43
M6993	7 oz.	51	M14940	8 oz.	31-49	M20859A	2½ lbs.	49
M6994	7 oz.	51	M14949	1 lb.	43	M21138	1½ lbs.	43
M7013	2¼ lbs.	41	M14950	15 oz.	43	M21273A	5½ lbs.	49
M7016	1½ oz.	51	M14980	2 oz.	47	M21274A	2½ lbs.	49

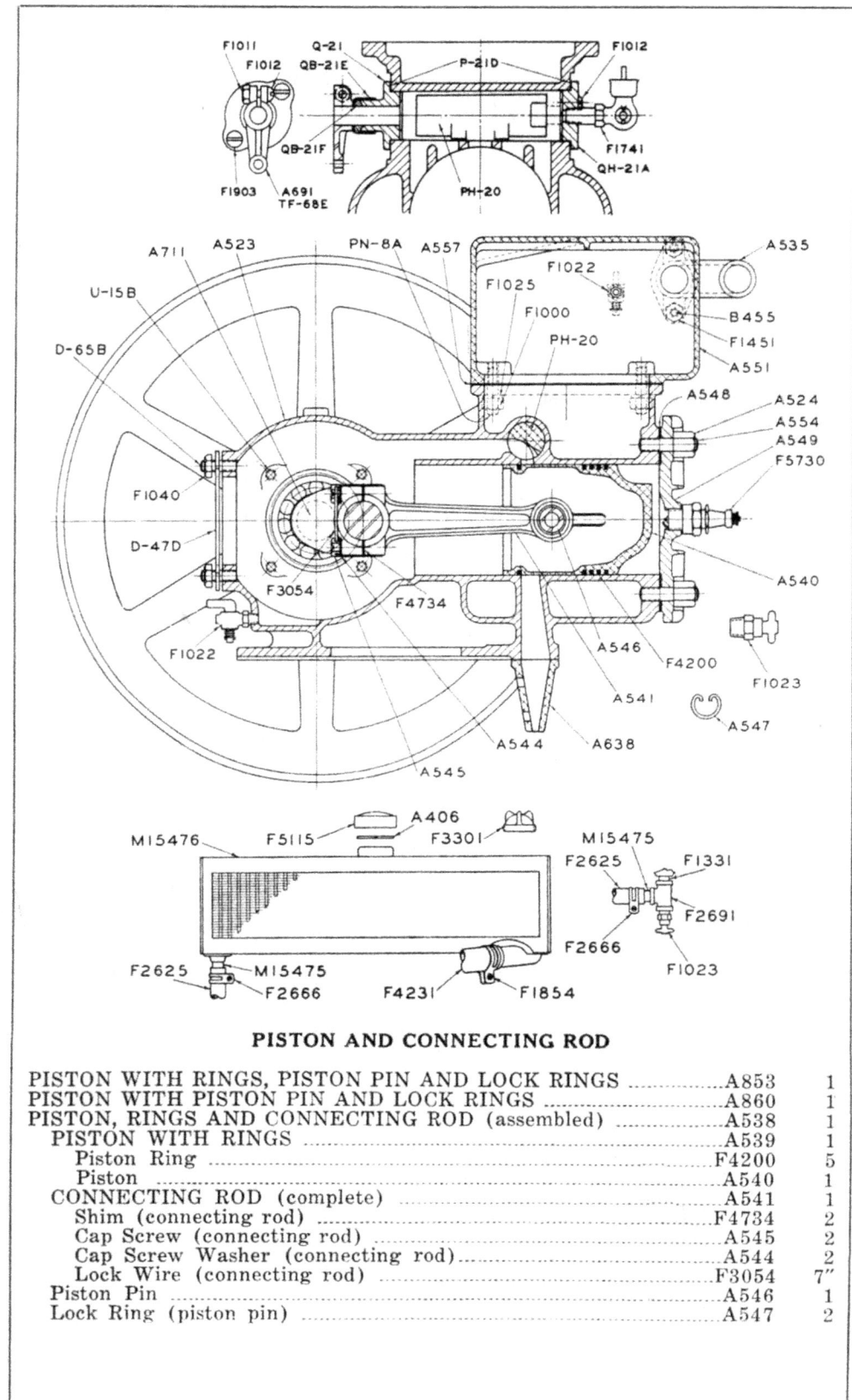

PISTON AND CONNECTING ROD

PISTON WITH RINGS, PISTON PIN AND LOCK RINGS	A853	1
PISTON WITH PISTON PIN AND LOCK RINGS	A860	1
PISTON, RINGS AND CONNECTING ROD (assembled)	A538	1
PISTON WITH RINGS	A539	1
Piston Ring	F4200	5
Piston	A540	1
CONNECTING ROD (complete)	A541	1
Shim (connecting rod)	F4734	2
Cap Screw (connecting rod)	A545	2
Cap Screw Washer (connecting rod)	A544	2
Lock Wire (connecting rod)	F3054	7"
Piston Pin	A546	1
Lock Ring (piston pin)	A547	2

Bulletin 294A—Page 29
Fairmont M19 Car—Series C

CYLINDER AND CRANKCASE

CYLINDER AND CRANKCASE WITH STUDS	A764	1
CYLINDER AND CRANKCASE WITH THROTTLE VALVE	A522	1
CYL. AND CRANKCASE WITH STUDS AND THROTTLE VALVE	A765	1
Cylinder and Crankcase	A523	1
Stud (side bearing)	U-15B	8
Stud (cylinder head)	A554	6
Stud (carburetor)	D-65B	2
Throttle Valve	PH-20	1
Guide (throttle valve)	Q-21	1
Cover (throttle valve)	QH-21A	1
Screw (throttle guide and cover)	F1903	4
Screw (throttle stop)	F1012	1
Gasket (throttle guide and cover)	P-21D	2
Packing (throttle stem)	QB-21F	1
Packing Cup (throttle)	QB-21E	1
THROTTLE ARM, SCREW AND NUT	TF-268-2	1
Throttle Valve Arm	TF-68E	1
Screw (throttle valve arm)	F1012	1
Nut (throttle valve arm screw)	F1011	1
Priming Cup	F1741	1
Drain Cock (crankcase)	F1022	1
Cylinder Head	A549	1
Gasket (cylinder head)	A548	1
Nut (cylinder head stud)	A524	6
Gasket (carburetor to crankcase)	D-47D	1
Nut (carburetor stud)	F1040	2
Muffler	A638	1
Machine Bolt 3/8 x 1½ (muffler—not ill.)	F1024	2
Lock Washer 3/8 (muffler bolt—not ill.)	F1025	2
Nut 3/8 hex (muffler bolt—not ill.)	F1000	2

WATER JACKET AND COOLING SYSTEM

WATER JACKET (with flanged elbow)	A550	1
Water Jacket (bare)	A551	1
Cock (water level)	F1022	1
Stud 5/16 x 1-1/8	B455	2
Gasket (elbow—not ill.)	A534	1
Elbow (for condenser hose)	A535	1
Nut 5/16	F1451	2
Lock Washer 5/16	F1100	2
Stud 3/8 x 1-5/8	PN-8A	4
Gasket (jacket to cylinder)	A557	1
Nut (water jacket stud)	F1000	4
Lock Washer (water jacket stud)	F1025	4
Name Plate (not ill.)	F3607	1
Pin (name plate—not ill.)	F1013	4
Guard Rail (for condenser—ill. with housing on page 50)	M14886	1

NOTE—Late cars have condenser filler caps of the bayonet type, while early ones were of the screw thread type. When ordering, select proper cap.

CONDENSER (with bayonet type cap)	M15476	1
FILLER CAP (bayonet type)	F5115	1
Gasket (filler cap)	A406	1
Filler Cap (screw thread type—for early cars)	F3301	
Machine Bolt 5/16 x 3/4	F1489	4
Lock Washer 5/16	F1100	4
Pipe Nipple 3/8	F1331	1
Pipe Tee 3/8	F2691	1
Drain Cock (water jacket)	F1023	1
Hose Nipple 3/8	M15475	2
Hose 1¼ (for steam)	F4231	19"
Hose Clamp 1¼	F1854	2
Hose 5/8 (for return)	F2625	22"
Hose Clamp 5/8	F2666	2
Overflow Hose (not ill.)	F3006	16"

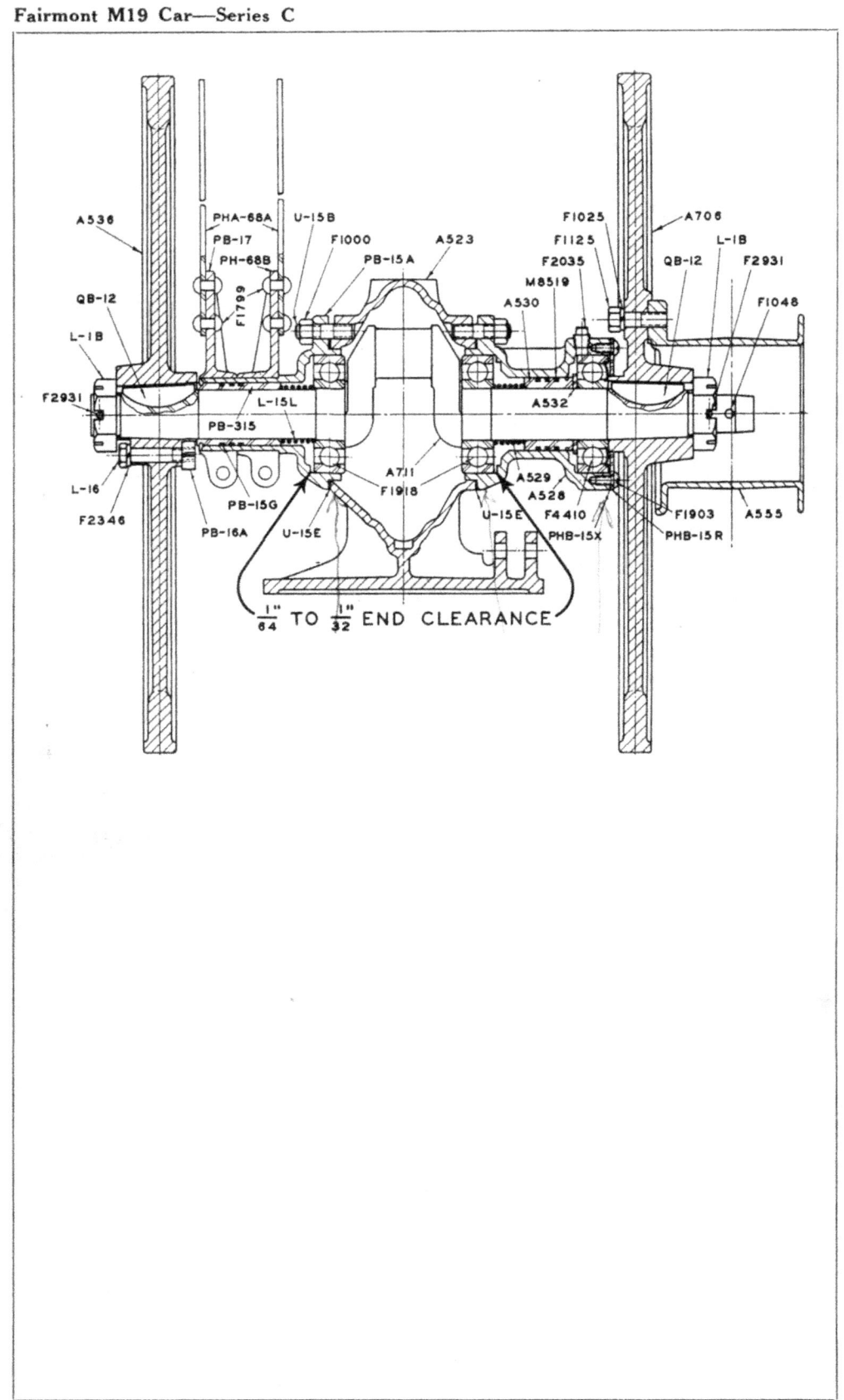

FLYWHEELS—CRANKSHAFT—SIDE BEARINGS

NOTE—For engines No. 45367 and higher order belt flywheel A706 and crankshaft A711. Earlier engines were fitted with belt flywheel A537 and crankshaft A527. Separate parts should not be interchanged between the two groups. We recommend application of A706 and A711, together when belt flywheel or crankshaft is needed for earlier engines.

Part	Number	Qty
Flywheel (timer or magneto side)	A536	1
Flywheel (belt side—see note)	A706	1
Flywheel (belt side—see note)	A537	1
Key (flywheel)	QB-12	2
Nut (flywheel)	L-1B	2
Cotter (flywheel nut)	F2931	2
CRANKSHAFT WITH BALL BEARINGS (see note)	A712	1
Crankshaft (see note)	A711	1
Ball Bearing	F1918	2
CRANKSHAFT WITH BALL BEARINGS (see note)	A526	1
Crankshaft (see note)	A527	1
Ball Bearing	F1918	2
Ball Bearing (outboard)	F4410	1
Gasket (side bearing)	U-15E	2
Stud (side bearing)	U-15B	8
Nut (side bearing stud)	F1000	8
Side Bearing (timer side)	PB-15A	1
PACKING SLEEVE WITH RINGS (timer side)	PB-315	1
Packing Ring (timer side)	PB-15G	3
Spacer Spring (timer side)	L-15L	1
Side Bearing (belt side)	A528	1
Pipe Plug (belt side bearing)	F2035	1
PACKING SLEEVE WITH RINGS (belt side)	A530	1
Packing Ring (belt side)	M8519	3
Spacer Spring (belt side)	A529	1
Washer (outboard bearing)	A532	1
Cover (belt side bearing)	PHB-15R	1
Gasket (cover)	PHB-15X	1
Screw (cover)	F1903	4

STARTING CRANK

Part	Number	Qty
Pin (starting crank)	F1048	1
Starting Crank (ill. on page 4)	M16420	1
Steady Bearing (starting crank—ill. on page 48)	M14940	1
Machine Bolt 5/16 x 1	F1099	2
Lock Washer 5/16	F1100	2

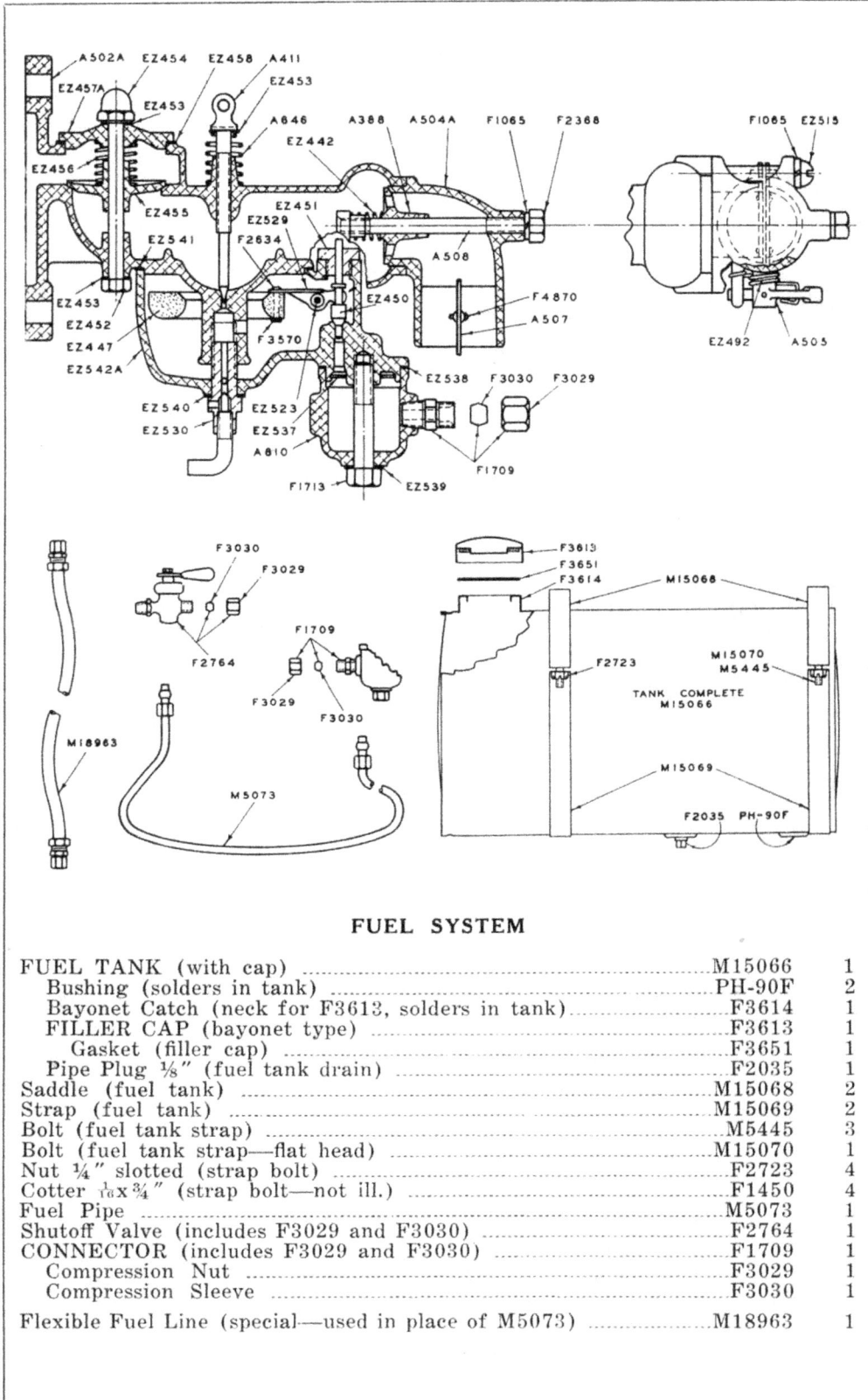

FUEL SYSTEM

FUEL TANK (with cap)	M15066	1
Bushing (solders in tank)	PH-90F	2
Bayonet Catch (neck for F3613, solders in tank)	F3614	1
FILLER CAP (bayonet type)	F3613	1
Gasket (filler cap)	F3651	1
Pipe Plug ⅛" (fuel tank drain)	F2035	1
Saddle (fuel tank)	M15068	2
Strap (fuel tank)	M15069	2
Bolt (fuel tank strap)	M5445	3
Bolt (fuel tank strap—flat head)	M15070	1
Nut ¼" slotted (strap bolt)	F2723	4
Cotter ₁⁄₁₆ x ¾" (strap bolt—not ill.)	F1450	4
Fuel Pipe	M5073	1
Shutoff Valve (includes F3029 and F3030)	F2764	1
CONNECTOR (includes F3029 and F3030)	F1709	1
Compression Nut	F3029	1
Compression Sleeve	F3030	1
Flexible Fuel Line (special—used in place of M5073)	M18963	1

CARBURETOR

Part	Number	Qty
Gasket (carburetor to crankcase—ill. page 28)	D-47D	1
Nut (carburetor stud—ill. page 28)	F1040	2
CARBURETOR (complete)	A642	1
Carburetor Body	A502A	1
Carburetor Bowl	EZ542A	1
Gasket (bowl to body)	EZ541	1
Drain Cock (complete)	EZ530	1
Gasket (drain cock)	EZ540	1
CORK FLOAT WITH LEVER	EZ528	1
Float	EZ447	1
Float Lever with Bearing	EZ529	1
Washer (float screw—not ill.)	EZ526	1
Float Screw	F2634	2
Float Screw Nut	F3570	2
Float Lever Pin	EZ523	1
Float Valve	EZ450	1
Guide (float valve)	EZ451	1
Check Valve Stem with Lower Nut	EZ452	1
Gasket (check valve stem)	EZ453	2
Check Valve Stem Nut (upper)	EZ454	1
Check Valve	EZ455	1
Spring (check valve)	EZ456	1
Cover (check valve)	EZ457A	1
Gasket (check valve cover)	EZ458	1
Needle Valve	A411	1
Friction Washer (needle valve)	EZ453	1
Friction Spring (needle valve)	A646	1
AIR VALVE CAGE WITH CHOKE	A503A	1
Cage (air valve)	A504A	1
Stem (air valve)	A508	1
Spring (air valve)	EZ442	1
Air Valve	A388	1
Lock Washer ¼" (air valve stem)	F1065	1
Nut (air valve stem)	F2368	1
Choke Arm and Shaft	A505	1
Choke Spring	EZ492	1
Choke Disc	A507	1
Choke Disc Screw (self tapping)	F4870	2
Screw (air valve cage)	EZ515	2
Lock Washer ¼" (air valve cage screw)	F1065	2
STRAINER BOWL (includes connector)	A810	1
CONNECTOR (includes F3029 and F3030)	F1709	1
Screen (strainer)	EZ537	1
Gasket (strainer bowl)	EZ538	1
Cap Screw (strainer bowl)	F1713	1
Gasket (strainer bowl screw)	EZ539	1

Page 34—Bulletin 294A
Fairmont M19 Car—Series C

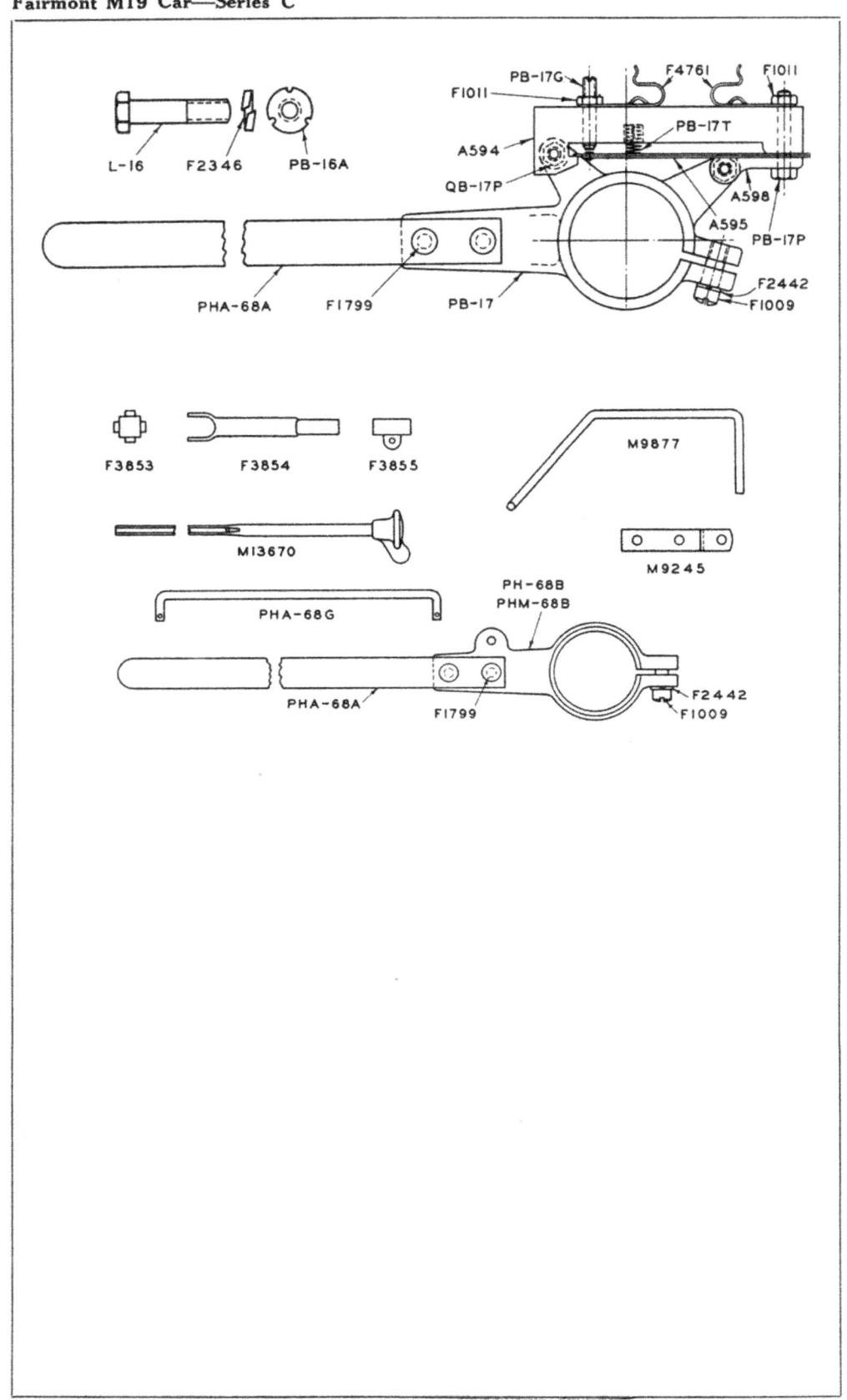

TIMER

Wiping Block	PB-16A	1
Bolt (wiping block)	L-16	1
Lock Washer ⅜	F2346	1
TIMER COMPLETE	A355	1
TIMER LEVER (assembled)	A662	1
Timer Casting	PB-17	1
Handle (only)	PHA-68A	1
Rivet ¼ x ½	F1799	2
Clamp Screw	F1009	1
Lock Washer 5/16	F2442	1
TIMER BLOCK WITH POINTS	A593	1
Timer Block	A594	1
Timer Blade (with point)	A595	1
Spring (timer blade)	PB-17T	1
Ground Block	A598	1
Screw (timer blade)	PB-17P	1
Nut (timer screw)	F1011	2
Connector	F4761	2
Adjusting Screw (with point)	PB-17G	1
Mounting Screw (timer)	QB-17P	2

CARBURETOR CONTROL

Universal Spider	F3853	1
Adjustable Rod Sleeve	F3854	1
Adjusting Rod	M13670	1
Choke Sleeve	F3855	1
Choke Wire (not ill.)	F3054	11"

THROTTLE CONTROL

THROTTLE LEVER (complete—battery engines only)	PHA-268	1
Casting (only—width 1⅛")	PH-68B	1
THROTTLE LEVER (complete—magneto engines only)	PHMA-268	1
Casting (only—width ⅞")	PHM-68B	1
Handle	PHA-68A	1
Rivet ¼ x ½	F1799	2
Clamp Screw	F1009	1
Lock Washer 5/16	F2442	1
Throttle Rod	PHA-68G	1
Cotter 3/32 x ½	F1027	2

MAGNETO CONTROL PARTS

Support Clip (control rod—Bosch)	M9245	1
Control Rod (Bosch)	M9877	1
Support Bracket (control rod—Eisemann—not ill.)	M19104	1
Control Rod (Eisemann—not ill.)	M19105	1
Machine Screw 12-24 x ¾	F1008	
Nut 12-24	F1011	
Cotter 3/32 x ½	F1027	

Page 36—**Bulletin 294A**
Fairmont M19 Car—Series C

Bulletin 294A—Page 37
Fairmont M19 Car—Series C

BATTERY IGNITION EQUIPMENT

NOTE—Late cars have coil and batteries in the same box, while early ones had coil in tool box and a shorter battery box. The improved box M16490 is applicable to early cars by following instructions sent with it.

BATTERY BOX (with coil spacer)	M16490	1
Battery Box (less cover)	M16489	1
Cover (battery box)	M16496	1
Coil Spacer	M16495	1
Clamp Bolt	F4258	2
Wing Nut (clamp bolt)	F1053	2
Step Bolt 1/4 x 7/8 (holds battery box)	F2610	2
Lock Washer 1/4	F1065	2
Dry Cell	F1081	4
Spark Coil (F3419 without bracket)	F4756	1
Vibrator (both points included)	F4166	1
Connector (battery)	M2314	3
Spark Plug	F5730	1
Spark Plug Wire (with terminals)	M16492	1
Switch	F1421	1
Wood Screw No. 6x3/4	F1082	2
Wire (switch to timer—23")	M17112	1
Wire (switch to coil—49")	M16493	1
Wire (battery to timer—72")	M16491	1
Wire (coil to battery—13")	M16642	1
Cable Clip (fiber)	C-48	3
Wood Screw No. 9x5/8	F1387	2
Nut 1/4 stove bolt	F2712	1
Washer 3/16	F1050	3
High Tension Wire (per foot)	F1402	
Primary Wire (per foot)	F2958	

HEADLIGHT

HEADLIGHT (with bracket and bolts)	M8404	
Mounting Bracket	M8403	
Headlight Bulb	F3300	
Reflector	F403	
Lamp Socket with Wires	F405	
Dry Cell	F1081	
LENS and CLAMP RING (cemented together)	F4179	
Lens	F400	
Clamp Ring	F402	
Lens Gasket (copper asbestos)	F401	
Switch	F404	
Handle with Screws	F4180	

TOOLS

TOOL KIT (in bag)	M16354	1
Draw String Bag	M6738	1
Ball Pein Hammer	F2945	1
6" Pliers	F2946	1
3" Screw Driver	F2948	1
Connecting Rod Socket Wrench	F4413	1
End Wrench 7/16 x 1/2	F2950	1
End Wrench 9/16 x 5/8	F2951	1
End Wrench 3/4 x 13/16	F2952	1
Oil Can	F2966	1
End Wrench 7/8 x 1	F3741	1
9" Adjustable Wrench	F2947	1

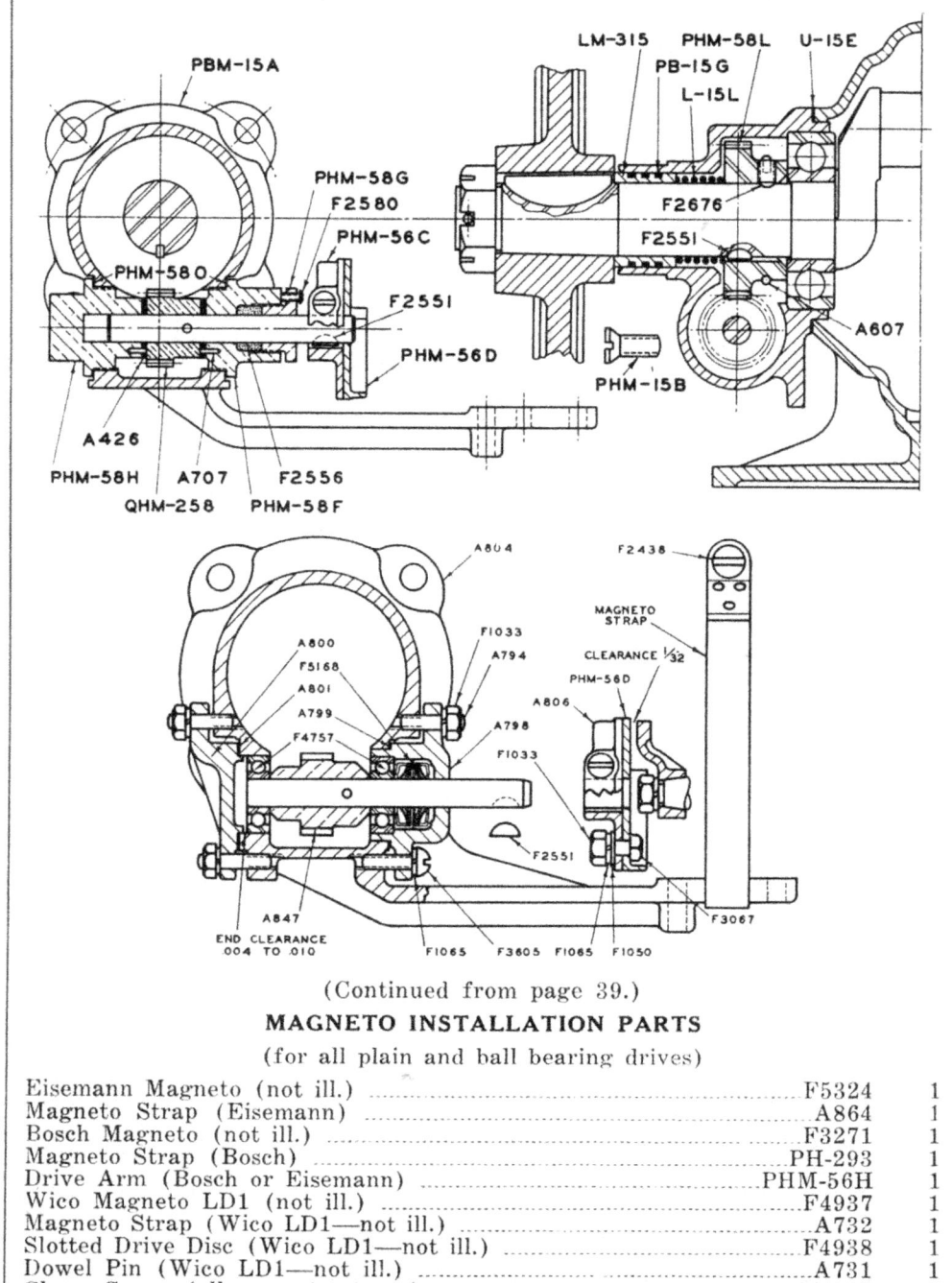

(Continued from page 39.)

MAGNETO INSTALLATION PARTS

(for all plain and ball bearing drives)

Eisemann Magneto (not ill.)	F5324	1
Magneto Strap (Eisemann)	A864	1
Bosch Magneto (not ill.)	F3271	1
Magneto Strap (Bosch)	PH-293	1
Drive Arm (Bosch or Eisemann)	PHM-56H	1
Wico Magneto LD1 (not ill.)	F4937	1
Magneto Strap (Wico LD1—not ill.)	A732	1
Slotted Drive Disc (Wico LD1—not ill.)	F4938	1
Dowel Pin (Wico LD1—not ill.)	A731	1
Clamp Screw (all magneto straps)	F2438	1
Cap Screw ¼ x ¾ (holds magneto—not ill.)	F1064	3
Cap Screw ¼ x 1½ (holds magneto—not ill.)	F2608	1
Clamp Screw (all drive discs)	F1009	
Cap Screw ¼ x ⅝	F3067	
Wrot Washer	F1050	
Nut ¼	F1033	
Lock Washer ¼	F1065	
Lock Washer	F1100	
Lock Washer ⅜	F1025	

NOTE—Engines below No. 45800 had plain bearing magneto drive shafts, while later ones have shafts mounted in ball bearings. The ball bearing group can be applied to earlier engines, by ordering assembly A803, F2551 key, and either the A805 or A807 coupling.

BALL BEARING MAGNETO DRIVE

SIDE BEARING with DRIVE SHAFT (assembled)	A803	1
Side Bearing (ball bearing drive)	A804	1
DRIVE SHAFT with GEAR and BALL BEARINGS	A795	1
Drive Shaft with Gear	A847	1
Ball Bearing	F4757	2
Cover (closed)	A800	1
Gasket (for closed cover)	A801	1
Cover (for oil seal)	A798	1
Gasket (for oil seal cover)	A799	1
Oil Seal	F5168	2
Cover Stud	A794	3
Nut ¼	F1033	3
Screw ¼ x ¾	F3605	1
Lock Washer ¼	F1065	4
MAGNETO COUPLING (assembled) (Bosch or Eisemann)	A805	1
Drive Disc (with screw)	A806	1
Driving Gap	PHM-56D	1
MAGNETO COUPLING (assembled) (Wico LD1—not ill.)	A807	1
Drive Disc (with screw)	A806	1
Drive Plate (with studs—not ill.)	A719	1

PLAIN BEARING MAGNETO DRIVE

NOTE—Side bearing PBM-15A for the plain bearing magneto drive is no longer furnished, but all parts listed below are available. When a PBM-15A side bearing is required, order assembly A803, F2551 key, and either the A805 or A807 coupling.

Drive Shaft with Gear	QHM-258	1
Gasket (drive shaft bearing)	PHM-58O	2
DRIVE SHAFT BEARING (closed end)	PHM-58H	1
DRIVE SHAFT BEARING (for packing)	PHM-58F	1
Thrust Washer	A426	2
Pin (thrust washer)	A707	6
Packing (preformed metallic)	F2556	1
Packing Nut	PHM-58G	1
Lock Screw (packing nut)	F2580	1
MAGNETO COUPLING (assembled) (Bosch or Eisemann)	PHM-256	1
Drive Disc (with screw)	PHM-56C	1
Driving Gap	PHM-56D	1
MAGNETO COUPLING (assembled) (Wico LD1—not ill.)	A726	1
Drive Disc (with screw)	PHM-56C	1
Drive Plate (not ill.)	A719	1

MAGNETO INSTALLATION PARTS

(for all plain and ball bearing drives)

NOTE.—For magneto spare parts see bulletin 202.

Crankshaft Gear	PHM-58L	1
Gear Set Screw	F2676	1
Lock Ring	A607	1
Key	F2551	2
Set Screw Wrench (not ill.)	F3032	1
Flat Head Screw ⅜ x 1	PHM-15B	2
PACKING SLEEVE with RINGS	LM-315	1
Packing Ring	PB-15G	3

(Continued at bottom of page 38.)

Page 40—**Bulletin 294A**
Fairmont M19 Car—Series C

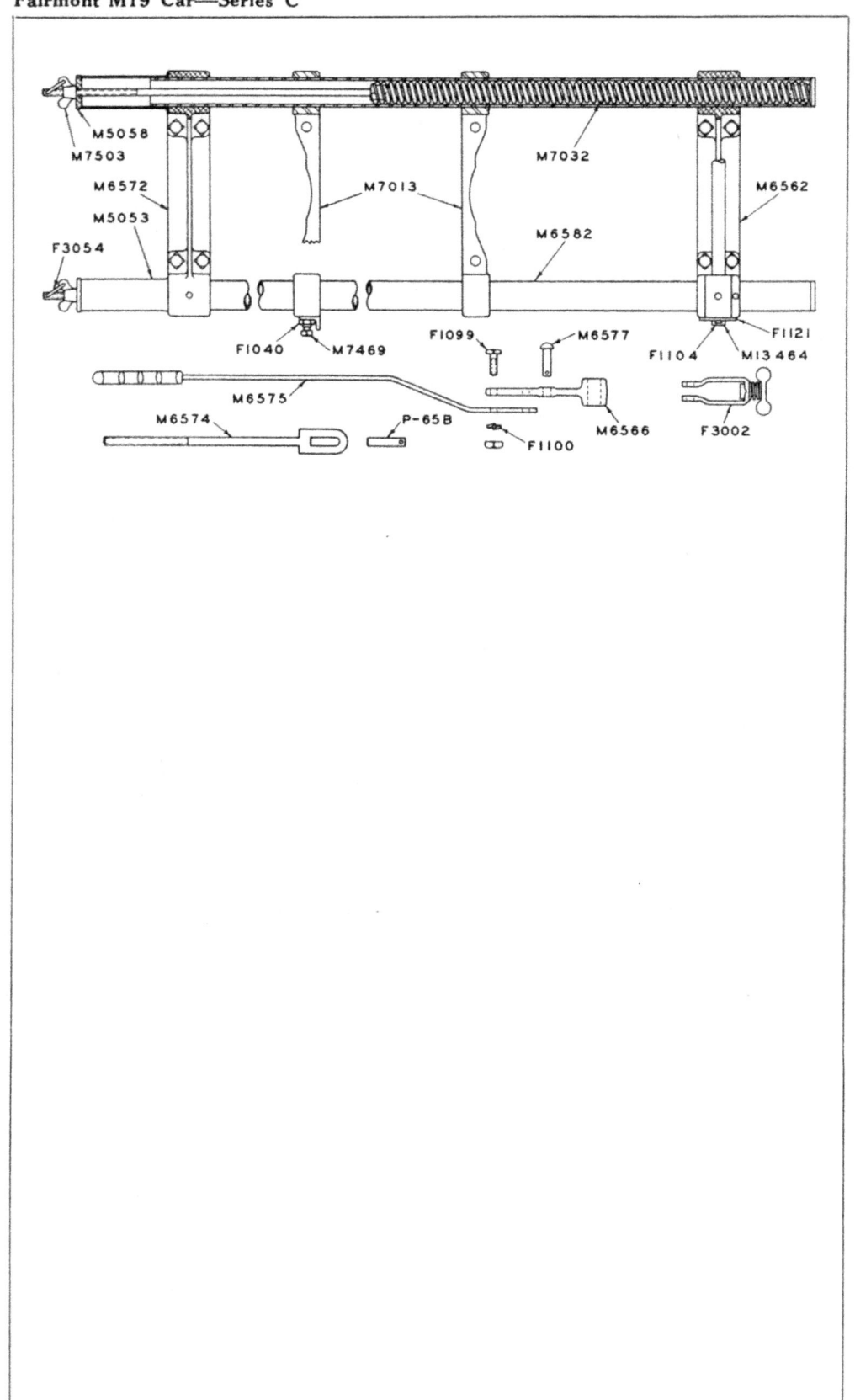

SLIDING BASE

Bearing (sliding base—front)	M6572	1
Bearing (sliding base—rear)	M6562	1
Machine Bolt ⅜ x 1½	F1024	6
Machine Bolt ⅜ x 4½	F2690	2
Support Tube (engine)	M6582	2
Engine Support	M7013	2
Set Screw ⅜ x 1 (special)	M7469	4
Nut ⅜	F1040	4
Tension Spring Assembly (parts not sold separately)	M7032	2
Tension Tube (front)	M5053	2
Tube End (front cover)	M5058	2
Wing Nut (tension spring)	M7503	2
Lock Wire	F3054	1 ft.
Pull Rod (sliding base)	M6574	1
Pin (pull rod)	P-65B	1
Adjuster (pull rod—yoke and wing nut)	F3002	1
Pin (pull rod adjuster)	M6577	1
Shaft (sliding base lever)	M13464	1
Wrot Washer ⅝	F1121	2
Socket (sliding base lever)	M6566	1
Lever (sliding base)	M6575	1
Machine Bolt 5/16 x 1	F1099	2
Cotter ⅛ x 1	F1104	3
Cotter 3/32 x 1	F1882	1
Lock Washer ⅜	F1025	8
Lock Washer 5/16	F1100	2

ENGINE AND MOUNTING

Engine (battery)	O	
Engine (magneto)	OM	
Machine Bolt 7/16 x 1½	F1428	4
Nut 7/16 (hex)	F1029	4
Lock Washer 7/16	F4160	4

BELT—PULLEYS

NOTE—For illustrations of axle pulley parts see page 42, and engine pulley parts page 30.

Endless Cord Belt 3x62" (ill. on page 48)	F3000	1
Engine Pulley 4"	A555	1
Cap Screw (use F1025 lock washer)	F1125	3
AXLE PULLEY (with bolts)	M13536	1
Axle Pulley (less bolts)	M13537	1
Machine Bolt ⅜ x 2 (use F1025 lock washer)	F1640	4
Nut ⅜ hex	F1000	4
Drive Key (axle pulley)	M3639	1

Page 42—**Bulletin 294A**
Fairmont M19 Car—Series C

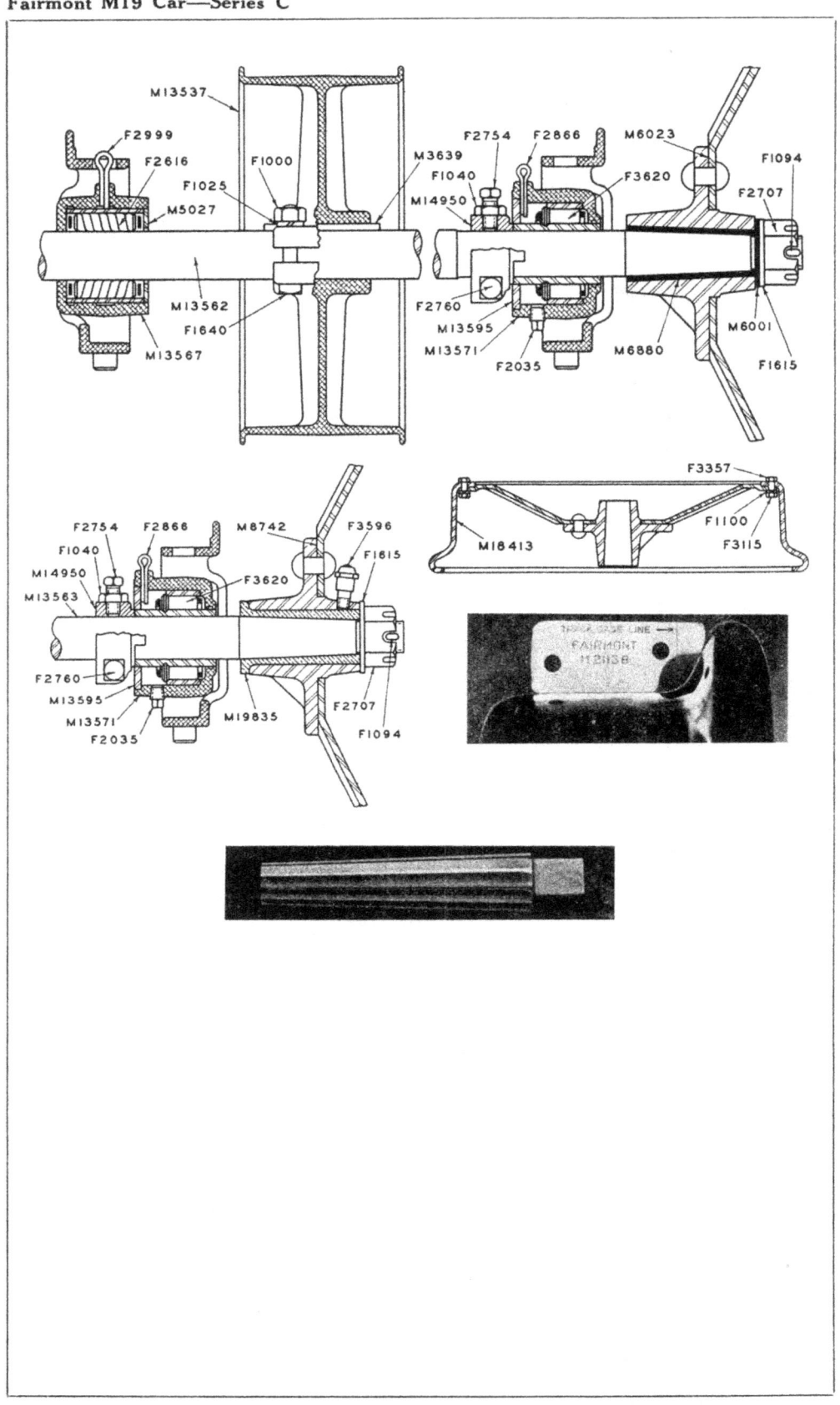

For axle bearing parts, see pages 44, 45.

AXLES—THRUST COLLARS

Drive Axle	M13562	1
Loose Axle	M13563	1
Axle End Nut	F2707	4
Cotter (Axle end nut)	F1094	4
THRUST COLLAR 1 3/16" (complete)	M14949	4
Thrust Collar	M14950	4
Clamp Bolt (thrust collar)	F2760	4
Lock Washer 3/8	F1025	4
Set Screw (thrust collar)	F2754	4
Nut 3/8 half	F1040	4

WHEELS—INSULATION—LOOSE WHEEL BUSHING

NOTE.—Complete wheels, and hub and disc assemblies, do not include insulation or loose wheel bushing. Always order extra, if required.

17"x1/4" TWO PIECE WHEEL (taper bored for insulation)	M19866	3
Hub and Disc (taper bored for insulation)	M6023	3
17"x1/4" TWO PIECE WHEEL (loose—straight bored)	M19868	1
Hub and Disc (straight bored—with oiler)	M8742	1
Oiler (for loose wheel)	F3596	1
17"x1/4" Wheel Tire	M18413	4
TIRE BOLT SET (12 each bolt, nut, lock washer)	M19874	4
Tire Bolt (heat treated)	F3357	48
Lock Washer 5/16	F1100	48
Nut 5/16 hex SAE	F3115	48
INSULATION 1 3/16" (complete)	M6334	3
Insulating Bushing	M6880	3
Insulating Washer	M6001	3
Steel Washer	F1615	3
Loose Wheel Bushing (filleted shoulder—late cars)	M19835	1
Loose Wheel Bushing (square shoulder—early cars—not ill.)	M8697	1
Washer (steel—loose wheel)	F1615	1
Taper Hand Reamer (for wheels and insulation)	M7666	
Shock Wheel Puller (for pulling wheels—not ill.)	M8705	
Wheel Gauge (for checking wheel gauge)	M21138	

Page 46—Bulletin 294A
Fairmont M19 Car—Series C

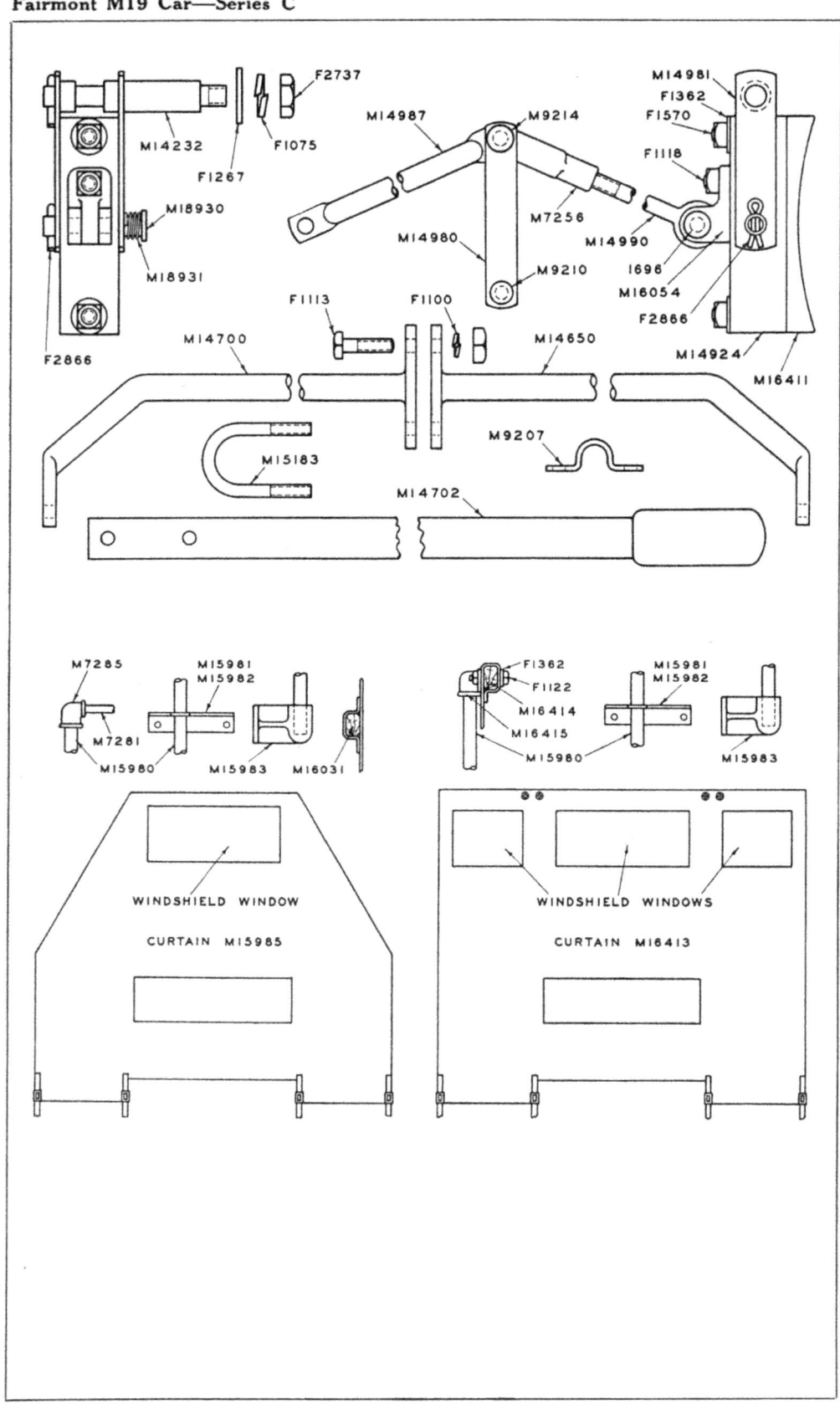

Bulletin 294A—Page 47
Fairmont M19 Car—Series C

BRAKE

NOTE—Each brake shoe on late cars is firmly held between the hanger links by a friction spring and long hanger pin. These parts are applicable to early cars which used plain short hanger pins without springs. Order one each of M18930, M18931, and F2866 cotter for each shoe.

A few early cars had asbestos lined brake shoes, but these have been superseded with metal lined ones, which are interchangeable.

Part	Number	Qty
Brake Lever (with grip)	M14702	1
Brake Shaft (right half)	M14650	1
Brake Shaft (left half)	M14700	1
Machine Bolt 5/16 x 1 1/4	F1113	2
Bearing (center—U Bolt)	M15183	1
Nut 5/16	F1114	4
Bearing (outer)	M9207	2
Machine Bolt 5/16 x 3/4	F1489	4
Link (toggle)	M14980	4
Pin (toggle link—5/16 x 7/8)	M9210	2
Pin (toggle arm to link—3/8 x 1 1/4)	M9214	2
Pivot Stud	M14232	4
Lock Washer 1/2	F1075	4
Wrot Washer 1/2	F1267	4
Nut 1/2 hex	F2737	4
Toggle (non adjustable)	M14987	2
ADJUSTABLE TOGGLE (assembled)	M14988	2
Yoke	M7256	2
Eye Bolt	M14990	2
BRAKE SHOE WITH LINER (assembled)	M16432	4
Brake Shoe (block only)	M14924	4
Claw	M16054	4
Carriage Bolt 5/16 x 1 1/2	F1118	4
Liner	M16411	4
Machine Bolt 5/16 x 1 3/4	F1570	8
Wrot Washer 5/16	F1362	8
Pin (brake shoe claw)	1696	4
Shoe Hanger	M14981	8
Hanger Pin	M18930	4
Spring	M18931	4
Cotter 3/16 x 1	F2866	8
Cotter 1/8 x 3/4	F1030	6
Cotter 3/32 x 3/4	F1076	2
Lock Washer 5/16	F1100	6

WINDSHIELDS

Part	Number	Qty
WINDSHIELD (complete—standard)	M15984	1
Windshield Curtain (with window)	M15985	1
Top Cross Bar	M7281	1
Top Socket	M7285	2
Cross Bar (center—wood)	M16031	1
WINDSHIELD (complete—wide three window)	M16412	1
Windshield Curtain (with windows)	M16413	1
Top Cross Bar	M16414	1
Top Socket	M16415	2
Machine Bolt 5/16 x 1 1/2	F1122	4
Washer 5/16 wrot	F1362	4

The following items are common to both groups.

Part	Number	Qty
Bracket (left—bolts to guard rail)	M15981	1
Bracket (right—bolts to guard rail)	M15982	1
Vertical Post	M15980	2
Lower Socket	M15983	2
Machine Bolt 5/16 x 1 (use eight F1100 lock washer)	F1099	8

Fairmont M19 Car—Series C

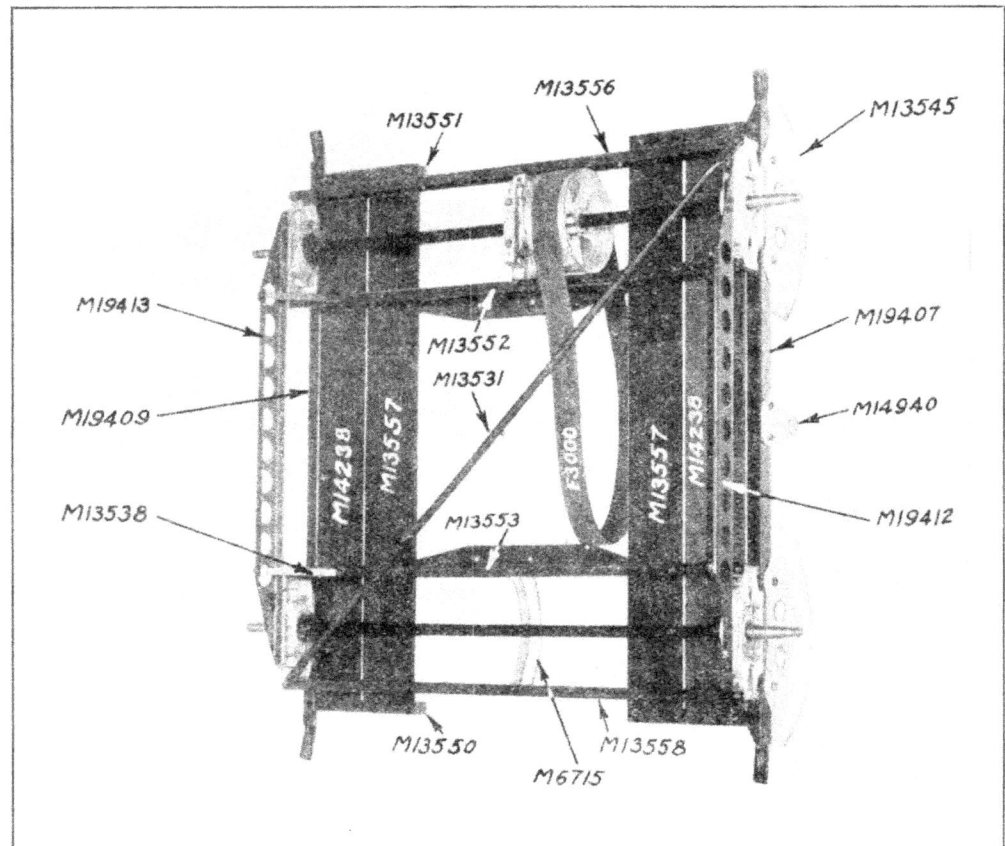

Bulletin 294A—Page 49
Fairmont M19 Car—Series C

FRAME AND DECK

NOTE—Side rails and rail skids used on cars below serial No. 138714 are no longer furnished, as these parts do not have clearance for the long bearing guides now standard. When using new style rail skids M19412 and M19413 with old installations having short guides, insert strips of thin sheet metal between rail skids and under side of bearing supports M13564 to close the openings. New style side rails M19407 and 19409 used with short guide installations must be equipped with protecting covers M19406.

When applying long guide bearings to early cars, side rails and rail skids must either be cut away to provide clearance, or replaced with new style ones, and protecting covers used. Also see note under axle bearings on page 44.

Part	Number	Qty
Cross Channel No. 1 (no. from FRONT of car)	M13558	1
Cross Channel No. 2 (with engine support)	M13553	1
Cross Channel No. 3 (with engine support)	M13552	1
Cross Channel No. 4 (rear)	M13556	1
Front Center Casting	M6715	1
Sway Brace	M13531	1
Machine Bolt ⅜x3½	F1511	8
Machine Bolt ⅜x3¾	F2721	2
Machine Bolt ⅜x4½	F2690	2
Machine Bolt 5/16x1½	F1122	2
Side Rail (right—with handles)	M19407	1
Side Rail (left—with handles)	M19409	1
Cover (bearing guide—illustrated on page 44)	M19406	8
Machine Bolt ⅜x1½	F1024	8
Wheel Guard	M13545	4
Machine Bolt ⅜x1	F1159	8
Rail Skid (right)	M19412	1
Rail Skid (left)	M19413	1
Machine Bolt ⅜x1¼	F1318	8
Brace (rail skid)	M13538	4
Machine Bolt 5/16x¾	F1489	8
Deck Floor Board (inside)	M13557	2
Deck Floor Board (outside—notched)	M14238	2
Step Bolt 5/16x1	F2872	16
Deck End Block (high)	M13550	3
Deck End Block (low)	M13551	1
Carriage Bolt 5/16x4	F1867	6
Carriage Bolt 5/16x2½	F1108	2
Carriage Bolt 5/16x3¾	F3076	1
Carriage Bolt 5/16x2	F1101	1
Grip Washer (square) 5/16	F3071	10
Wrot Washer 5/16	F1362	8
Nut 5/16	F1114	10
Lock Washer 5/16	F1100	26
Lock Washer ⅜	F1025	34
Steady Bearing (starting crank—listed with crank)	M14940	

WIDE WHEEL GUARDS AND STEP PLATES

NOTE—These parts can be supplied as extra equipment on new cars at the factory. Step plates can be applied in the field to standard series C cars with 17" wheels, by drilling four extra holes in each side rail. Wide wheel guards interchange with standard ones, no drilling required.

Part	Number	Qty
Wheel Guard (wide)	M16675	4
STEP PLATES (set of two with bolts)	M21273A	1
Step Plate (left)	M20859A	1
Step Plate (right)	M21274A	1
Machine Bolt 5/16x1	F1099	8
Machine Bolt 5/16x1¼	F1113	2
Lock Washer 5/16	F1100	10

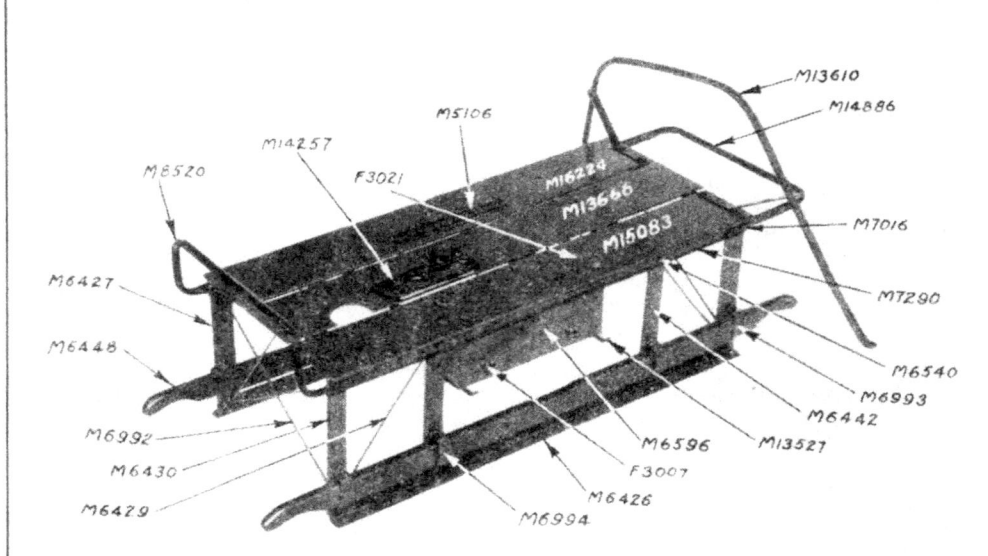

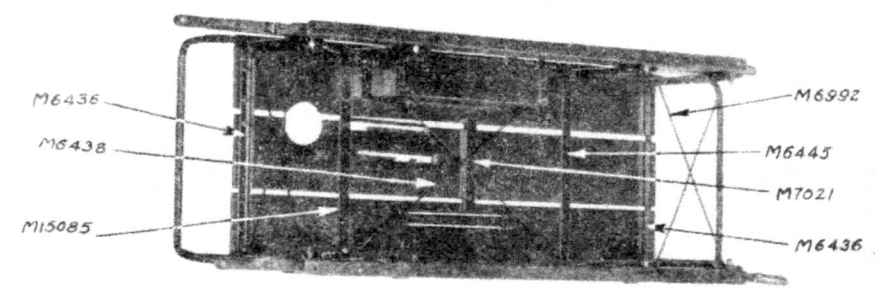

EXTENSION LIFT HANDLES

EXTENSION LIFT HANDLE (complete)	M7035	2
Handle (only)	M6448	2
Screw (flat head)	F1112	4
Wrot Washer ⅜	F1115	4
Nut ⅜ hex	F1040	4
Clip (handle)	M6472	4
Wood Screw No. 9 x 1	F2431	4

HOUSING

Part	Number	Qty
Outside Guide (lift handle)	M6993	4
Inside Guide (lift handle)	M6994	4
Machine Bolt 3/8 x 3/4	F2887	8
Safety Rail (front—complete with braces)	M13610	1
Machine Bolt 5/16 x 1	F1099	4
Hand Rail (rear)	M8520	1
Machine Bolt 3/8 x 1	F1159	2
Guard Rail (condenser—front)	M14886	1
Machine Bolt 5/16 x 3/4	F1489	2
Side Channel (lower)	M6426	2
Side Channel (top left—not ill.)	M6428	1
Side Channel (top right)	M7290	1
Vertical Channel (right front—left rear)	M6427	2
Vertical Channel (left front—right rear)	M6430	2
Vertical Channel (left middle—not ill.)	M7157	2
Vertical Channel (right middle)	M6442	2
Side Brace (1/4 rod)	M6429	4
End Brace (1/4 rod)	M6992	4
Diagonal Brace (top—5/16 rod)	M6438	2
Cross Strap (top—middle front)	M6445	1
Cross Strap (top—middle rear)	M15085	1
End Cross Angle (top—front and rear)	M6436	2
Bolt 1/2 x 1 3/8 (SAE—drilled)	M6540	12
Bolt 1/2 x 1 (SAE—drilled)	M7016	4
Wrot Washer 1/2	F1267	4
Nut 1/2 (SAE castle)	F1702	16
Cotter 3/32 x 1	F1882	16
Seat Board (right)	M15083	1
Seat Board (middle)	M13666	1
Cleat (wood—middle seat board)	M7021	1
Wood Screw No. 9 x 1	F2431	2
Seat Board (left—for battery cars)	M16224	1
Seat Board (left—for magneto cars)	M15084	
Step Bolt 1/4 x 3/4	F2906	14
Step Bolt 1/4 x 7/8	F2610	4
Guide (brake and sliding base levers)	M14257	1
Guide (throttle and timer levers)	M5106	2
Stove Bolt 1/4 x 1 (flat head)	F3069	3
Stove Bolt 1/4 x 1 (round head)	F1627	3
Stove Bolt 1/4 x 1 1/2 (round head)	F1685	1
Wrot Washer 1/4	F1106	7
Nut 1/4 Stove Bolt	F2712	7
TOOL BOX (with cover)	M6592	1
Box (only)	M6594	1
COVER (with hinges)	M6596	1
Spring Hinge	F3007	2
Hasp (for tool box cover)	M7289	1
Rivet 3/16 x 1/4	F1793	2
Muzzle Snap (for tool box cover)	F3039	1
Step Bolt 1/4 x 8	F3021	4
Bracket (starting crank)	M13527	2
Nut 1/4	F2700	4
Guard (flywheel—not ill.)	M7036	1
Step Bolt 1/4 x 3/4	F2906	2
Lock Washer 1/4	F1065	20
Lock Washer 5/16	F1100	6
Lock Washer 3/8	F1025	10
Chassis Bolt 3/8 x 3/4 (drilled—housing to frame)	M7187	8
Slotted Nut 3/8	F2877	8
Cotter 3/32 x 1	F1882	8
Machine Bolt 5/16 x 4 (front safety rail to frame)	F1601	2
Nut 5/16	F1114	2

BOLTS—NUTS—WASHERS—SCREWS

These items are grouped, and listed by size for convenience in ordering. All bolt and nut threads are U. S. standard, unless otherwise specified.

MACHINE BOLTS

F1489	5/16 x 3/4
F1099	5/16 x 1
F1113	5/16 x 1 1/4
F1122	5/16 x 1 1/2
F1570	5/16 x 1 3/4
F1601	5/16 x 4
F2887	3/8 x 3/4
F1159	3/8 x 1
F1318	3/8 x 1 1/4
F1024	3/8 x 1 1/2
F1640	3/8 x 2
F2760	3/8 x 2 1/4
F1511	3/8 x 3 1/2
F2721	3/8 x 3 3/4
F2690	3/8 x 4 1/2
F1428	7/16 x 1 1/2

CARRIAGE AND STEP BOLTS

F2906	1/4 x 3/4 Step
F2610	1/4 x 7/8 Step
F4258	1/4 x 4 1/4
F3021	1/4 x 8 Step
F2872	5/16 x 1 Step
F1118	5/16 x 1 1/2
F1101	5/16 x 2
F1108	5/16 x 2 1/2
F3076	5/16 x 3 3/4
F1867	5/16 x 4

STOVE BOLTS

F3069	1/4 x 1 Flat Hd.
F1627	1/4 x 1 Rd. Hd.
F1685	1/4 x 1 1/2 Rd. Hd.

NUTS

F3570	No. 2-56 Hex
F1011	No. 12-24 Hex
F2712	1/4 Stove Bolt
F2368	1/4 Hex Half
F1033	1/4 Hex
F2723	1/4 Hex Slotted
F2700	1/4 Square
F1053	1/4 Wing
F1451	5/16 Hex
F3115	5/16 Hex S. A. E.
F1114	5/16 Square
F1040	3/8 Hex Half
F1000	3/8 Hex
F2877	3/8 Hex Slotted
F1029	7/16 Hex
F2737	1/2 Hex Half
F1702	1/2 Hex S. A. E. Castle

WASHERS

F1050	5/16 Wrot
F1065	1/4 Lock-positive type
F1106	1/4 Wrot
F1100	5/16 Lock-positive type
F2442	5/16 Lock-special
F1362	5/16 Wrot
F3071	5/16 Square Grip
F1025	3/8 Lock-positive type
F2346	3/8 Lock
F1115	3/8 Wrot
F4160	7/16 Lock
F1075	1/2 Lock-positive type
F1267	1/2 Wrot
F1121	5/8 Wrot

SCREWS

F2634	2-56 x 3/4 Rd. Hd. Machine
F2580	10-24 x 3/8 Rd. Hd. Machine
F1012	12-24 x 5/8 Rd. Hd. Machine
F1008	12-24 x 3/4 Rd. Hd. Machine
F1903	14-20 x 1/2 Rd. Hd. Machine
F3067	1/4 x 5/8 Hex Hd. Cap
F3605	1/4 x 3/4 Rd. Hd. Cap
F1064	1/4 x 3/4 Hex Hd. Cap
F2608	1/4 x 1 1/2 Hex Hd. Cap
F1009	5/16 x 3/4 Fillister Head
F1713	5/16 x 1 3/4 Hex Hd. Cap
F1125	3/8 x 1 1/4 Hex Hd. Cap
F2438	3/8 x 1 1/2 Fillister Head
F1112	3/8 x 1 1/2 Flat Hd. Cap
F1082	No. 6 x 3/4 Flat Hd. Wood
F1387	No. 9 x 5/8 Rd. Hd. Wood
F2431	No. 9 x 1 Flat Hd. Wood

COTTERS

F1450	1/16 x 3/4
F1027	3/32 x 1/2
F1076	3/32 x 3/4
F1882	3/32 x 1
F1030	1/8 x 3/4
F1104	1/8 x 1
F2931	3/32 x 1 1/2
F2866	3/16 x 1
F1094	3/16 x 1 1/4
F2999	1/4 x 1

MISCELLANEOUS

F3054	Lock Wire
F2035	1/8 Pipe Plug
F1013	Escutcheon Pin
F1048	No. 5 x 1 1/4 Taper Pin
F2912	No. 5 x 1 3/4 Taper Pin
F1793	3/16 x 1/4 Rivet
F1799	1/4 x 1/2 Rivet

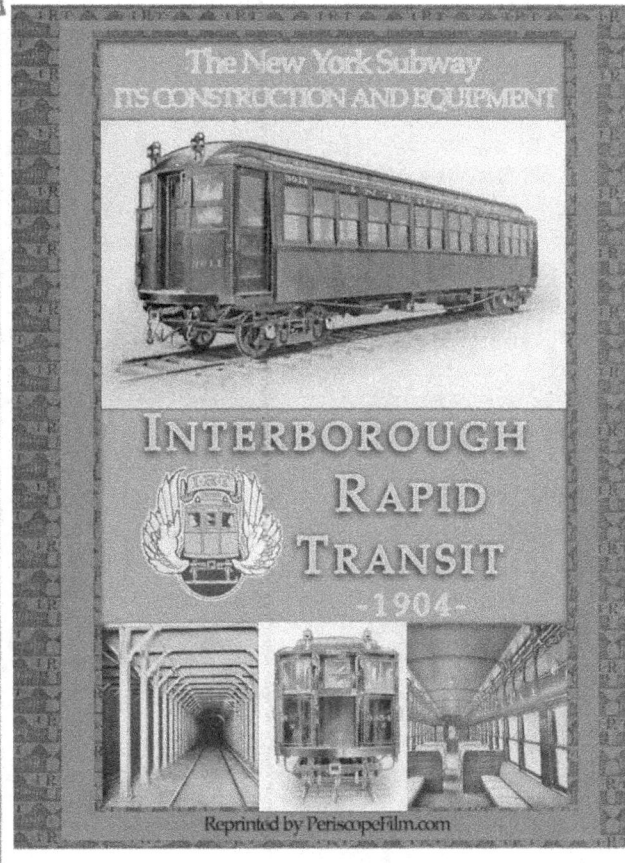

On October 27, 1904, the Interborough Rapid Transit Company opened the first subway in New York City. Running between City Hall and 145th Street at Broadway, the line was greeted with enthusiasm and, in some circles, trepidation. Created under the supervision of Chief Engineer S.L.F. Deyo, the arrival of the IRT foreshadowed the end of the "elevated" transit era on the island of Manhattan. The subway proved such a success that the IRT Co. soon achieved a monopoly on New York public transit. In 1940 the IRT and its rival the BMT were taken over by the City of New York. Today, the IRT subway lines still exist, primarily in Manhattan where they are operated as the "A Division" of the subway. Reprinted here is a special book created by the IRT, recounting the design and construction of the fledgling subway system. Originally created in 1904, it presents the IRT story with a flourish, and with numerous fascinating illustrations and rare photographs.

Originally written in the late 1900's and then periodically revised, A History of the Baldwin Locomotive Works chronicles the origins and growth of one of America's greatest industrial-era corporations. Founded in the early 1830's by Philadelphia jeweler Matthais Baldwin, the company built a huge number of steam locomotives before ceasing production in 1949. These included the 4-4-0 American type, 2-8-2 Mikado and 2-8-0 Consolidation. Hit hard by the loss of the steam engine market, Baldwin soldiered on for a brief while, producing electric and diesel engines. General Electric's dominance of the market proved too much, and Baldwin finally closed its doors in 1956. By that time over 70,500 Baldwin locomotives had been produced. This high quality reprint of the official company history dates from 1920. The book has been slightly reformatted, but care has been taken to preserve the integrity of the text.

NOW AVAILABLE AT
WWW.PERISCOPEFILM.COM

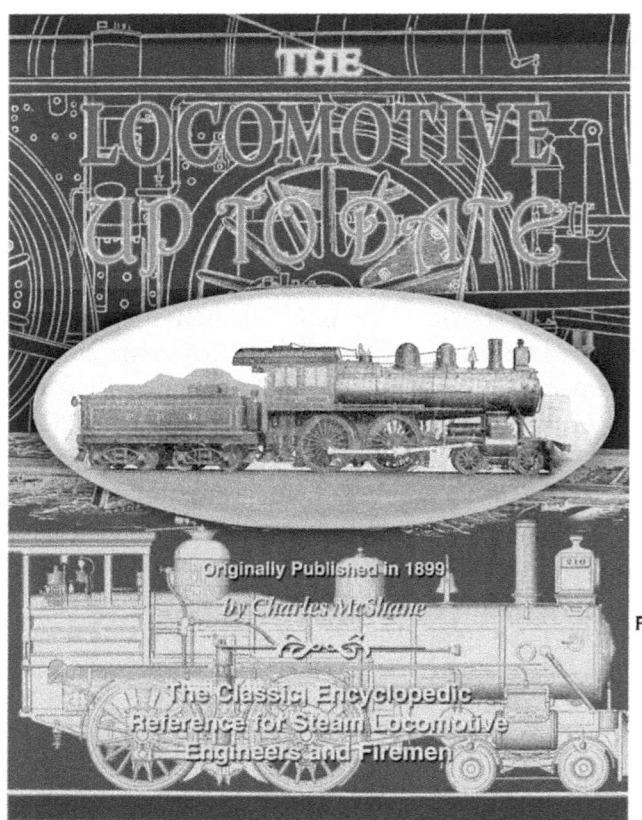

When it was originally published in 1899, **The Locomotive Up to Date** was hailed as "...the most definitive work ever published concerning the mechanism that has transformed the American nation: the steam locomotive." Filled with over 700 pages of text, diagrams and photos, this remains one of the most important railroading books ever written. From steam valves to sanders, trucks to side rods, it's a treasure trove of information, explaining in easy-to-understand language how the most sophisticated machines of the 19th Century were operated and maintained. This new edition is an exact duplicate of the original. Reformatted as an easy-to-read 8.5x11 volume, it's delightful for railroad enthusiasts of all ages.

Originally printed in 1898 and then periodically revised, **The Motorman...and His Duties** served as the definitive training text for a generation of streetcar operators. A must-have for the trolley or train enthusiast, it is also an important source of information for museum staff and docents. Lavishly illustrated with numerous photos and black and white line drawings, this affordable reprint contains all of the original text. Includes chapters on trolley car types and equipment, troubleshooting, brakes, controllers, electricity and principles, electric traction, multi-car control and has a convenient glossary in the back. If you've ever operated a trolley car, or just had an electric train set, this is a terrific book for your shelf!

ALSO NOW AVAILABLE FROM PERISCOPEFILM.COM!

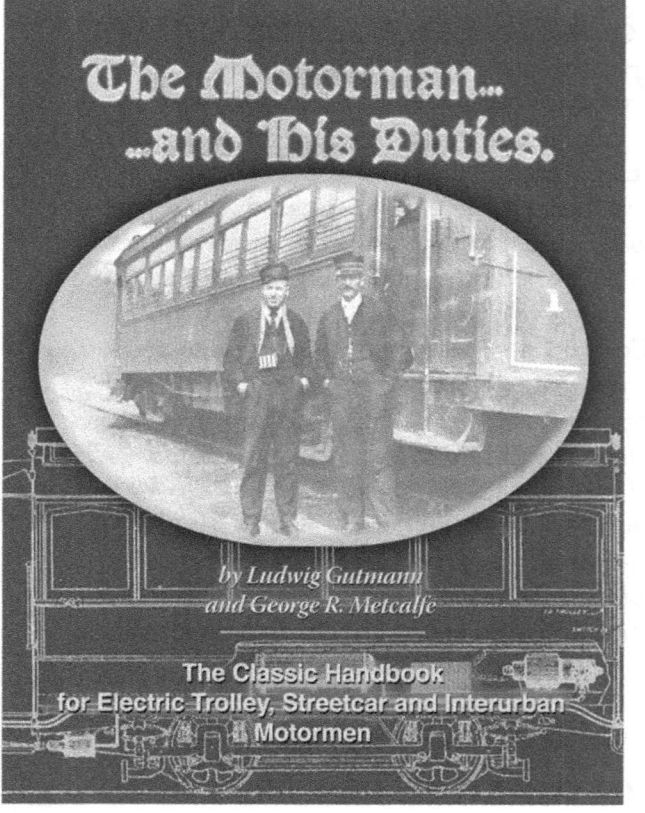

THE CLASSIC 1915 TROLLEY CAR AND INTERURBAN RAILWAY BOOK

ELECTRIC RAILWAY ENGINEERING

By Francis H. Doane, A.M.B.

REPRINTED BY PERISCOPEFILM.COM

©2010 Periscope Film LLC
All Rights Reserved
www.PeriscopeFilm.com

ISBN # 978-1-935700-23-4

www.ingramcontent.com/pod-product-compliance
Lightning Source LLC
Chambersburg PA
CBHW081356040426
42451CB00017B/3470